Wooden Spoon
ANNIVERSARY
RUGBYWORLD
Yearbook 2010

Editor

Ian Robertson

Photographs

Getty Images

GreenUmbrella
Publishing

This book has been produced for Green Umbrella Publishing
by Lennard Books
a division of Lennard Associates Ltd
Windmill Cottage
Mackerye End
Harpenden
Herts AL5 5DR

This edition first published in the UK in 2009
by Green Umbrella Publishing

www.gupublishing.co.uk

Paperback   ISBN 978-1-907311-33-8
Hardback   ISBN 978-1-907311-34-5

Production Editor: Chris Marshall
Design Consultant: Paul Cooper
Jacket Design: Kevin Gardner
Printed and bound in Britain by Butler Tanner & Dennis

The publishers would like to thank Getty Images for providing most of the photographs for this book. The publishers would also like to thank Nigel Chanter/sportactionphotos.co.uk, Fotosport UK, Huw Evans, Matthew Impey, Raechelle Inman, Inphopics, Penguin International RFC, Chris Thau and Wooden Spoon for additional material.

Contents

EVEN GREATER TOGETHER

HSBC

PRINCIPAL PARTNER

HSBC Rugby Festivals are uniting over 60,000 children across England, Ireland, Scotland, Wales and South Africa. If you'd like to know more on how HSBC is helping the Lions of the future to become even greater together, visit www.lionsrugby.com/hsbc

Investing in youth rugby for the future of the Lions.

FOREWORD

by HRH THE PRINCESS ROYAL

BUCKINGHAM PALACE

HRH The Princess Royal,
Royal Patron of Wooden Spoon.

The game of rugby has changed much over the last 25 years but the one constant factor in this development of the game has been the continuing growth and effectiveness of Wooden Spoon, the Charity of British and Irish rugby.

Wooden Spoon was founded after England's disappointment on the rugby pitch in 1983. Since then, Spoon has gone from strength to strength investing many resources into easing the hardships of children and young people disadvantaged in life.

Rugby is a game of great commitment requiring energy, enthusiasm and skill that are translated into a physically demanding and invariably exciting spectacle. The volunteers, members and supporters of Wooden Spoon bring the same attributes to their fundraising activities for the benefit of others.

As Wooden Spoon celebrates its 25th anniversary, we can look back with immense pride at its achievements and growth and in particular the number of children whose lives have been impacted because of the work of the Charity.

I wish everyone involved with Wooden Spoon success with their fundraising during this celebratory year and thank you for supporting a Charity that does so much to reflect the finest team game in the world.

Wooden Spoon

ANNIVERSARY

Evolution Not Revolution

by **SARAH GRIFFITHS**

Royal Patron: HRH The Princess Royal
Patrons: Rugby Football Union • Scottish Rugby Union • Welsh Rugby Union
Irish Rugby Football Union • Rugby Football League

We may be in the grip of a recession but that hasn't stifled Wooden Spoon's charitable work to improve the lives of disadvantaged young people. Spoon's two-year celebration of its 25th Anniversary draws to a close in 2010, and despite the economic climate Spoon is keeping its head well above water and learning to adapt itself very well to the situation.

In the UK, one child in every hundred suffers from a lifelong disability that will profoundly affect his or her ability to lead a full and happy life. More than 3.5 million young people grow up in

low-income households or live in an environment where they are subjected to poverty of aspiration. At Spoon, we believe that all children deserve the chance to live happy, fulfilled lives regardless of the challenges they may face. Spoon harnesses the spirit and values of rugby to give disadvantaged children and young people a chance to live happier, richer lives.

During our first 25 years, over half a million young people benefited from more than £15 million of support for charitable projects. These donations have diversified from capital projects such as medical centres, sports and activity areas, sensory rooms and gardens, playgrounds and hydrotherapy pools to include outreach programmes for young people in their communities. These new programmes are called Spoon Community Rugby (SCR) projects and are designed to give young people a better chance in life through playing rugby – a sport that channels their energy into healthy activity while fostering teamwork, discipline and respect.

Along with several new corporate sponsors and its principal supporter, TNT, Spoon has concluded its first year of SCR projects, and if the results are anything to go by then the programmes are proving to be a great success. Over the first year of activity, more than 20,000 children and young people have participated in one of the eight different SCR projects across the UK.

ABOVE Over 16,000 children from all over England have participated in the TRY Rugby programme since its launch at the Guinness Premiership curtain-raiser at Twickenham in September 2008.

FACING PAGE Onside project Ambassador Mike Tindall of Gloucester with youngsters who successfully graduated from the eight-week programme.

Try for Life

This programme consists of 24 projects being delivered by RFU coaches and Youth Offending Team staff to manage young people's anger and aggression, teaching discipline and respect in order to equip them for a life without criminal behaviour. The whole programme was funded by Spoon and Sport England.

One notable success has been in Nottingham, where none of the 20 participants had ever played rugby before. They had no clear understanding of how the game was played, or how to conduct themselves. They were disrespectful of their fellow participants and had trouble accepting decisions from the coaches. Over ten weeks the participants gelled as a group and began to enjoy participating in a team sport. The project was due to end with a celebratory final game against Northampton, but due to the enthusiasm shown, further fixtures have been arranged and a course has also been organised for the participants to gain a coaching qualification.

TRY Rugby

Health professionals estimate that the number of obese children is double that of ten years ago and that for these young people there is significant risk of health problems. Rugby has a proven track record of engaging kids of all builds, giving them a valuable role and avoiding the humiliation associated with many other sporting activities where being the wrong size or shape is a major impediment.

The TRY Rugby initiative was launched in September 2008 and was made possible through contributions from Spoon and Sport England through the National Sports Foundation. The programme is delivered by Premier Rugby across the 12 Guinness Premiership clubs and Bristol Rugby and the objectives are to increase activity in kids of all shapes and sizes, reduce childhood obesity levels, improve confidence and self-worth, improve physical and mental health and reduce bullying. Over 16,000 eight- to ten-year-old children from 260 schools in areas of greatest deprivation have been given the chance to try rugby.

England World Cup winner and Spoon Honorary President Lawrence Dallaglio put his support behind the campaign and explained, 'In any rugby team you will see a vast difference in the heights, weights and overall sizes of players. Just look at England's World Cup winning squad; Matt Dawson and Jonny Wilkinson are both about 5ft 10in and 13 stone, Steve Thompson is 6ft and was 18 stone and Martin Johnson is 6ft 7in and weighs 18 stone. They are all fit and very health-conscious but there is nearly a foot difference in their heights and five stone difference in their weights. Consequently rugby is the ideal vehicle to engage and motivate youngsters – they don't need to feel self-conscious about their size as rugby needs every shape and size in a team.'

Onside

Onside is the first SCR project to be developed directly with a Premiership club and a local young people's agency, Prospect Training, and recently won a prestigious Parliamentary Citizenship Award for Innovation. Championed by Mike Tindall and funded by TNT and Sport England, this project works with young people aged 16 to 18 in and around Gloucester who have no qualifications at all. The programme delivers rugby training with all the discipline, respect and teamwork that the game

brings to young people but in this case is wrapped up with key skills sessions with formal assessment work to be completed. The innovation in the programme is that the physical and skills training have been independently assessed to meet academic standards and by completing the course the young people get their first ever qualification. For some of the recent graduates, it has meant a whole new future: two joined the Army, three have secured part-time work at the club and two are being considered for volunteer coaching roles with the community team.

Mike Tindall, the Onside Ambassador, said, 'As a youngster there were plenty of distractions centred around anti-social behaviour – but through sport and rugby in particular, I found a drive and an energy to focus on something extremely positive in my life.

'If, in any way possible, I can provide encouragement, a positive role model and an ambassadorial role then I am delighted to do so. This scheme is vital to the young people of Gloucester and everyone has been working extremely hard to make it a success.'

Ospreys

This new project started in the summer of 2009 and works with young people who attend Pupil Referral Units (PRUs). These include young people who have either been excluded from mainstream school or so badly bullied in school that they are too terrified to attend.

Spoon commissioned Ospreys and the Enterprise Education Trust's business dynamics team to deliver a mixed programme of rugby skills and business enterprise skills. These life skills are linked to the commercial operations of a rugby club and other core skills like managing your personal finances.

LEFT A picture of concentration. Young rugby players from the TRY Rugby initiative provide half-time entertainment at Headquarters during the 2009 Guinness Premiership final between London Irish and Leicester Tigers.

LEFT AND FACING PAGE The Onside project, centred on Gloucester, combined academic and physical activities, including participants being put through their paces at the Cherry and Whites' ground at Kingsholm and by the Army at Chepstow.

Former Wales international Paul Thorburn is delighted to be the programme Ambassador and also for Spoon's support. 'Wooden Spoon has played a very significant and important role in getting this project started. In any environment there is always a shortage of funding for various projects. Thankfully we have managed to get this started with the help of Spoon.'

The first few sessions found some deeply disturbed and disinterested young people with no self-confidence or discipline. By the third session young people who had been completely silent thus far started to come out of their shells and are now fully participating.

In Touch

This is the first SCR project to be co-funded by Spoon regions (Worcester and West Midlands Regions), matched-funded by the central Spoon team and supported by Talbot Underwriting Ltd. The project works with young people with few or no qualifications and those who have been identified by local youth services as being at high risk of long-term unemployment.

The project works in two locations with young people from very different backgrounds: one group from rural Worcestershire, one group from central Birmingham. Both groups have difficult but different challenges, and this project aims to help each gain skills, respect and discipline, and to introduce life skills and new qualifications. In time the young people will swap locations to gain an understanding of the difficulties that the other group has to face and the means of overcoming them. They will then meet to share experiences and training, and to play competitive games against each other. Worcester Warriors Rugby Club is collaborating with Pertemps Coachright staff on the shared programme and providing role models and mentors from among their players for both groups of young people.

Additional projects

Rugby league in Scotland has an extremely good reputation for working in deprived areas in and around Glasgow with a track record of moving young people into positive activities around rugby. Spoon is working with the RL coaching staff to introduce physical skills and classroom sessions on healthy living, anger management and conflict resolution to nine- to 11-year-olds in the Glasgow area. The programme will use rugby to try and break the culture of judgment and conflict and engender respect and shared celebration of sporting activities. Twenty-six classes of 32 children are taking place over a five-week period with opportunities to participate in competitive mixed-denomination games against local schools.

In London, meanwhile, Spoon is working with The Crown Estate in Regent's Park to reduce anti-social and threatening behaviour by young people on housing estates in West Euston by providing them with positive replacement activity. The project runs two free open-access rugby sessions per week starting on the estates. Once confidence and trust has been built amongst the organisers, the sessions will be moved to Regent's Park, which borders the estates but which children have previously felt is not a place for them. The project is funded until 2010 thanks to The Crown Estate and Carter Jonas and in time it is hoped a permanent junior rugby club that is self-financing will be established to extend the benefits of the project in the future and to more young people.

The Contact Club is another great collaboration between a Spoon region (London) and Spoon central as well as a collaboration of two different sports. Launched in May 2009 in Hackney, East London, the programme comprises twice-weekly rugby and boxing training sessions for young men and women aged 13 to 19, particularly those who have very little to do and for whom boredom is often the cause of mischief and anti-social behaviour. Many of the participants wear tags and have anti-social behaviour orders to adhere to. The idea of mixing rugby and boxing is that both sports share many common training exercises; they also share the need for respect and discipline, while they meet different needs for individuals and teams.

Jason Leonard is Ambassador for both of the London projects and commented on his involvement, 'Last week I was running around in the pouring rain with fantastic kids from housing estates in Euston; the day after I was on my hands and knees in Hackney teaching kids from gangs how to scrummage. It is these results that make me proud to be a part of Wooden Spoon.'

Wooden Spoon is a wonderful charity that creates a positive impact in the lives of literally hundreds of thousands of children and young people. With the support of the Premiership clubs we have got overweight kids off the sofa and playing sport, with the support of the RFU we have worked with kids in youth offending units and given excluded teenagers a team game to play to prevent complete isolation. In South Wales we have worked with kids excluded from school to give them new discipline and ambition. These projects are prime examples of what can be achieved with a little imagination, some hard graft and the input of some very talented people. They help showcase the wonderful sport of rugby as a great vehicle for delivering new learning which can open up new horizons for the youth of today across the UK and Ireland.

Strutt&Parker&CountryHomes& Commercial&Farming&Land Management&BuildingSurveying &Leisure&Hotels&Development Land&Estate&FarmAgency& Accounting&Taxation&Planning& Development&Valuations& ResidentialDevelopment&Buying Service&RealEstateFinancial Services&SportingAgency& ResidentialSales&Lettings&proud supporters of the Wooden Spoon.

Strutt & Parker. The nationwide property specialist that offers a complete service through our network of over 45 offices.

www.struttandparker.com

COMMENT
& FEATURES

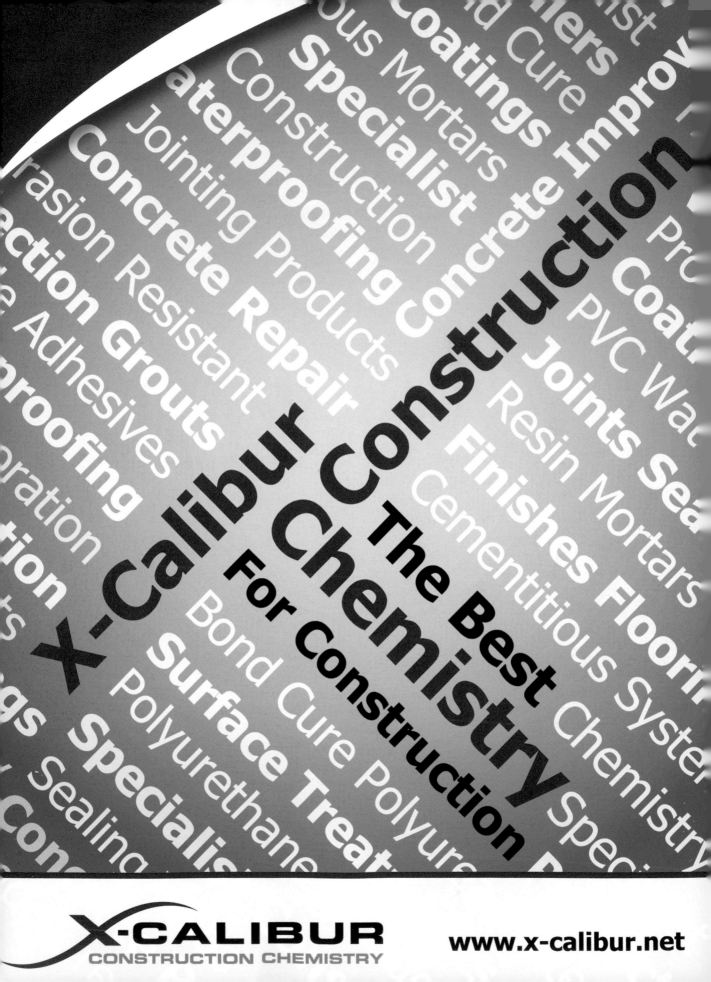

X-Calibur Construction Chemistry

The Best Chemistry For Construction

X-CALIBUR

CONSTRUCTION CHEMISTRY

www.x-calibur.net

James O'Connor the Story So Far ...

by RAECHELLE INMAN

"'I don't like to do comparisons, but obviously he has footwork that is not dissimilar to Christian Cullen. He has the ability to beat the man. He's a hard man to get a hold of'"

At the age of 18 years and 126 days, James O'Connor became the second youngest player to appear for the Wallabies when he was capped in the late stages of Australia's 30-20 win over Italy at Padova in November 2008.

'I only got on for about nine minutes but when I got on we were behind and we ended up winning the game and the feeling in the change room afterwards is something I haven't experienced before, it was amazing,' O'Connor said, reflecting on this momentous occasion.

O'Connor was an Australian Schools representative in 2007, and this boy wonder's rugby career took off quickly. 'The last two years have been a whirlwind. I wasn't expecting anywhere near what I have achieved so far,' he explained.

O'Connor made his first appearances for the Australian Sevens side in Hong Kong and Adelaide early in 2008 and this 'leapfrogged me into the Super 14 arena'. 'In the Sevens I improved and picked up so much confidence in myself; I knew that I could compete with some of the best attacking players in the world one

LEFT In the big time. Eighteen-year-old James O'Connor pictured during a training session on Australia's 2008 tour of Europe.

on one so I thought I had a good chance at Super 14. I just took it game by game and focused on learning from the guys around me,' said O'Connor of his baptism of fire.

Shortly after getting his break in the Sevens, O'Connor became the youngest ever debutant in Super 14 tournament history when he was sent on as a replacement for the Western Force against the Queensland Reds in Brisbane. Two weeks later his whole family flew from Brisbane to Perth to cheer him on in his first run-on game against the Chiefs. In a nail-biter, the Force won by a point, 22-21, thanks to an after-the-siren penalty from Matt Giteau. O'Connor contributed with some 'good touches' and finished his maiden Super rugby season with four caps. He then featured in every match on the Force's developmental tour of the United Kingdom.

O'Connor returned to Europe on the Wallabies spring tour where he ran on as a replacement in that match against Italy in Padova. He completed the tour with a stand-out performance against a star-studded Barbarians side at Wembley. 'When I found out that I was starting for the Wallabies at full back against the Barbarians words can't describe how good the feeling was. A day later the nerves kicked in when I found out who was in their back line ... they were the best players in the world. Then I had to put it in perspective, that I was getting the chance to play against these awesome players and it was such an opportunity to show what I was made of.'

O'Connor did make the most of his chances and it was that tour which convinced many that he was something special. Both of his tour appearances were made at No. 15, although he also plays at inside centre and fly half. In the 2009 Super 14 season, he impressed in the Force No. 12 shirt outside of Matt Giteau, but O'Connor also starred in two starts at full back midway through the competition. So now the teenage sensation has emerged as a solution to the Wallabies full back conundrum. In Australia's emphatic 55-7 victory over the Barbarians at Sydney in June, O'Connor came off the bench to replace Adam Ashley-Cooper at full back around an hour into the game, crossing for a try. He was then named at No. 15 in the starting line-up for the following Saturday's opening Test of the season against Italy at Canberra, in which he scored a hat-trick and was man of the match.

Other contenders for the full back position for Australia include Ashley-Cooper, Cameron Shepherd and Drew Mitchell, who all have experience, but it seems Wallabies coach Robbie Deans is preparing a side for the next Rugby World Cup and is leaning towards an exciting back-line combination of age and youth with skills and force.

Deans likes O'Connor's versatility, saying, 'Ultimately, he could settle into No. 12. He's clearly got the capacity to do that, and we'll clearly use him in that second-receiver role from No. 15. But in terms of day-in, day-out, week-in, week-out confrontation, he is not ready for that yet. From No. 15, it allows us to involve him, and It's where he can inject himself in the game in a way that suits.'

O'Connor says the extra space allows him to showcase his skills. 'The way Robbie [Deans] plays 15 is pretty much how I play 12, as a second ball player. You still get your hands on the ball a lot but you're a bit wider, so you get those one-on-one opportunities.' He says he can improve every aspect of his game, but at full back he is specifically focused on his field position and 'controlling' the defensive line.

O'Connor had originally been selected in the Australian Under 20 squad to play in the Junior World Championship in Japan in June 2009, but Deans had a rethink and was convinced O'Connor was now ready for a far bigger step – wearing the Wallabies No. 15 jersey and making his mark as a fully fledged international player. When asked why O'Connor had been promoted, Deans replied, 'It came down to James's performances, essentially. He's showed he is ready to push on. And we're ready to involve him. He warrants a start. We would not have contemplated retaining him if we weren't contemplating starting him. It's that simple.' O'Connor said that Deans told him he had been included in the Wallabies squad 'to fast-track my development'.

O'Connor has a strong rugby pedigree. His father, Warren, was born in Auckland and showed early promise, earning a spot in his school 1st XV at the tender age of 14, and played in representative teams before

FACING PAGE 'Rabbit' gets his kick in despite the intervention of Nick Koster as Australia defeat the Barbarians 18-11, this time at Wembley in November 2008.

BELOW James and friend meet HM The Queen at a reception at Windsor Castle in November 2008 to mark the centenary of the first Australian rugby tour to the British Isles.

he hung up his boots for good in his final year of school. James's grandfather Maurice represented Wellington. O'Connor's mother was also born in New Zealand, to South African parents, and his great-grandfather went close to representing the Springboks. So, in an unprecedented scenario, the utility back was eligible to represent rugby's three southern hemisphere powerhouses – Australia, New Zealand and South Africa. The Wallabies made sure he chose the country he grew up in.

It seems O'Connor has always excelled at sport – in athletics he was an 800m title holder in his age group; he represented Queensland at Australian Rules football in his first year in high school; and he even held scholarships with rugby league clubs from the age of 13, first with the Brisbane Broncos, then with the Parramatta Eels. James switched to rugby union when former Wallaby Paul Carozza picked him in a national rugby talent squad at 15 years of age. At Nudgee College, Brisbane's rugby nursery, O'Connor quickly attracted comparisons with Wallaby legend Tim Horan. It was at Nudgee that he got a taste for the rugby culture and the open, running game. 'I like to attack. I like to run the ball. If I see a hole I'll go for it, I won't play the safe option … I back myself,' he says with an abundance of confidence.

Like his current Australia team-mate Matt Giteau, he has a cheeky nature and is incredibly self-assured. 'The boys give me a bit of stick about being like Matt Giteau,' says O'Connor. It is obvious that he looks up to Giteau. 'I admire the way he holds himself on and off the field. From a rugby perspective he's got a complete game; he can kick, he can run, he can pass, he can tackle and he organises the team so well. It has been good learning outside of him.'

'Rabbit', as James has been known since his earliest RL days (he couldn't catch the ball yet aged five, but he already had a great sidestep), possesses slick ball skills and blinding acceleration. At

180cm (6ft) and 84kg (13st 3lbs), O'Connor is considered to be small in the current era of professionalism, but he has managed to establish himself as a reliable defender and is fast becoming thought of as a player who has the ability to have an immediate impact at the international level.

O'Connor is clearly an extrovert, with a twinkle in his eye and a mischievous smile, and describes himself as 'bubbly and easy-going'. He has a sense of adventure and likes being with people and constantly active. He is very close to his parents and two younger brothers. The teenager's goal is to cement a starting spot with the Wallabies and says his other dreams include winning a Super 14 and a World Cup. He will be only 21 when the Wallabies chase the Webb Ellis Cup in New Zealand in 2011.

Recently Deans, a former All Black Test full back, was asked if O'Connor reminded him of any other No. 15s. The Wallabies coach replied, 'I don't like to do comparisons, but obviously he has footwork that is not dissimilar to Christian Cullen. He has the ability to beat the man. He is not a big man, but he's a strong man, in terms of timing, balance and coordination. He's a hard man to get a hold of.'

O'Connor was 'stoked' that Deans had observed similarities to his childhood hero. 'Christian Cullen has been my favourite player since I first picked up a rugby ball. When my brothers and I played rugby in the backyard I was always Christian Cullen … it's an honour to be compared to such a great player.'

Deans concluded: 'He's got attributes that others have had, but there is only one O'Connor, so to speak.'

FACING PAGE O'Connor of the Western Force grabs Crusader Tim Bateman in the Super 14 round five clash in Christchurch in March 2009. James scored a try in the 23-23 draw.

BELOW In his first Test start in a Wallabies shirt, James crossed for three tries as Australia defeated Italy 31-8 at Canberra in June 2009.

Misce Stultitiam Consiliis Brevem

by PAUL STEPHENS

'The essence of this dispiriting tale concerns the west's big three. Bristol are no longer a Premiership club. By the end of last season they had been relegated'

BELOW Joe El Abd of Bristol and Bath's Michael Lipman at the launch of the 2008-09 Guinness Premiership. By the end of the season, Bristol had gone from the top flight, while Lipman's career seemed to be in tatters.

FACING PAGE Exeter Chiefs, who will play in the Championship in 2009-10, draw big crowds to their Sandy Park Stadium home.

You may not have noticed it, but the game in the West Country is in almost as much distress as the government. All three Premiership clubs, Bath, Bristol and Gloucester, have been vexed by assorted troubles, most of them of their own making. Smiles on the faces of the members of this disturbed threesome have been missing for too long. Is it any wonder?

Whatever the shame felt by the three clubs, it pales into insignificance at the way the national newspapers seem to have accorded in their desultory desire to ignore all those not in the Premiership, in terms of match reports, scorers and even tables. This discreditable treatment of all in National One (the Championship from 2009-10) is at least very embarrassing. Perhaps it is because the players from outside the top dozen clubs are not considered good enough to pull on an England jersey.

In mid-July of this year, Martin Johnson announced his selection, totalling 64 players. Called up for the Elite were 32, plus a similar number of Saxons. Nine of the former were from Leicester; five from London Wasps. In the Saxons line-up, five Leicester players have been included, with seven from High Wycombe club Wasps, who had not long before dispensed with their director of rugby, Lions coach Ian McGeechan. Thank you for all the good work you have done at Wasps, Ian.

Only five players overall were selected from northern clubs; none at all considered from promoted Leeds Carnegie or relegated Bristol. From National One not a single pick. With the game in the north of England in reasonably good shape where, one is entitled to ask, are the replacements for Bill Beaumont, Tony Neary, Jim Sydall, Mike Slemen, John Carleton, Fran Cotton, Peter Winterbottom, Steve Smith, Peter Squires and Roger Uttley? Have they all joined Leicester or Wasps, or perhaps signed up along with the bevy of overseas players now overwhelming the Premiership in England?

We like to think that rugby union in England is in good heart, but consider this: the British & Irish Lions party to South Africa this summer was selected with only eight England players on board. Tom Croft was eventually picked to replace the suspended Munster back-row forward Alan Quinlan to make it nine. Croft celebrated by scoring two tries during the opening Test in Durban.

The Ospreys from west Wales, without the endearingly self-conscious Gavin Henson, were represented by seven. True, the Ospreys have won two Celtic titles and the Anglo-Welsh Cup, but they have failed miserably in the Heineken Cup, like the remainder of the sides from the Principality, who have contested a solitary final; and that by Cardiff on home soil in 1995-96. Are England no better than the Ospreys? We shall see this winter. But to my mind the jury is still out on Martin Johnson, who pointedly refused to be drawn on Bath's questionable problems.

Exeter, Plymouth Albion and Penzance have been attracting increasing numbers to their stadia for home matches to rival those at Newcastle and Leeds. Exeter's new Sandy Park Stadium is

delightful, while Albion's Brickfields ground is a credit to all involved. Just what do they have to do to make the national newspapers? It could be worse, of course. They could have folded like Orrell and Wakefield, but that's another story.

The essence of this dispiriting tale concerns the west's big three. Bristol are no longer a Premiership club. By the end of last season they had been relegated and their head coach, former Bath and England scrum half Richard Hill, had departed for France, where he joins the division three club Chalon-sur-Saône, having spent six campaigns at the Memorial Stadium.

Hill, 48, is unrepentant about his decision, which comes ten seasons after the Bristol chairman, Arthur Holmes, sold the ground to Bristol Rovers of the Football League. If Rovers had not decided to proceed with another revamp of their Filton Avenue home, which was developed to accommodate rugby union in 1921, Bristol would have been obliged to move across the Severn to Newport and would be playing in the Championship at Rodney Parade for at least one season, if not two. What sort of appeal would they have had and what number of paying spectators would this have attracted?

The coaching at Bristol has fallen to a former player, Paul Hull, and his assistant, John Brain. But this is the third time that the famous old club has been relegated and a return to the Premiership is unlikely to be as seamless as Northampton's during their recent campaign. Exeter and Plymouth will join hands and want a say in that. In the short term, Hull has been busy with recruitment. James Merriman, a flanker, has joined from Neath; Cardiff scrum half Jason Spice has made the short journey to Bristol; Bertrand Bedes, Dan Montagu and Dan Norton make up a useful nap hand. We shall see.

With deserved applause for the new grandstand which signals a desire to redevelop Kingsholm ringing in the ears of the Gloucester board, as last season came to a close they chose to bring an end to Dean Ryan's contract as head coach. With a motor racing background, the chairman, Tom Walkinshaw, should need no reminding of the importance of speed. Yet Walkinshaw stands accused of being laggardly, for he did not appoint a director of rugby when Ryan was first engaged five years ago. Surely he will not be so disregarding now that Bryan Redpath has taken over from Ryan to work alongside forwards coach Carl Hogg or Denis Betts, the Kingsholm skills coach.

Meanwhile, Olly Barkley ended his miserable year at Gloucester and has returned to the Rec, with the addition to 23 England caps as his first aim. Signings to the Kingsholm playing assembly include new recruits Nicky Robinson from Cardiff and the Wasps winger Tom Voyce, plus Bath utility back Eliota Fuimaono-Sapolu.

Bath have been hogging the headlines of late. After receiving a two-year ban, the England prop Matt Stevens, who was found guilty of using cocaine, is off limits until January 2011. Stevens resigned. Club officials were then faced with an even bigger scandal when four first-team players were alleged to have participated in drug-taking at an end-of-season party, after they and Harlequins both lost their Premiership semi-finals. Bath lost to Leicester 24-10, while Quins were comprehensively defeated 17-0 by London Irish.

Harlequins were holding their annual fancy-dress bash at a west London bar when several Bath players arrived, having spent a long session at another venue in the north of the capital. The first casualty was Justin Harrison, the lock, who won 34 caps for Australia before joining Bath from Ulster on a one-year contract. He was soon on a plane back to Australia when the news broke. Subsequently he was banned for eight months after admitting a drug-taking charge.

Bath's chief executive, Bob Calleja, launched an inquiry into the behaviour of the other three players. They were Michael Lipman, Alex Crockett and Andrew Higgins who, it was alleged, all refused to take a drugs test on more than one occasion as part of an internal investigation. The trio then engaged a London solicitor, Richard Mallett, to represent them.

At the end of July, the three players, who have all quit the club, faced an RFU disciplinary hearing over their alleged refusals, under the general charge of 'conduct prejudicial to the interests of the game'. All three received a nine-month ban after a four-day meeting. At the time of writing, Lipman and Crockett were set to appeal; Higgins had announced his retirement.

Their coach, Steve Meehan, has plenty of work to do to paper over the cracks in Bath's facade. Three overseas players have been recruited: Luke Watson and Julian Salvi, both flankers, plus Matt Carraro, a Wallaby centre. They will be joined by David Wilson, a prop from Newcastle, and Ben Skirving, a back-rower from Saracens. Meanwhile, better news for the club is that scrum half Michael Claassens, capped by the Springboks eight times, has turned his back on South Africa to remain at the Rec.

The Roman poet and satirist Quintus Horace was on the button with his dictum *Misce Stultitiam Consiliis Brevem* – Mixing a Little Folly with Wisdom – which applies in spades to this disenchanted, dislocated trinity of clubs. There has been too much folly and insufficient wisdom, just as in the club game at large.

BELOW Alex Crockett, formerly a prominent member of the Bath club, scores against Bristol at the Rec in March 2009. His playing days may now be interrupted by a nine-month ban.

FACING PAGE Dean Ryan and Bryan Redpath by the posts at Adams Park, where Gloucester were playing Wasps. The 'Last Post' has sounded for Ryan. How long before a similar trumpet solo is heard for Redpath?

Birth of the Boks
the 1891 Tour of South Africa

by CHRIS THAU

'Maclagan's men won all 20 matches on tour, although South Africa battled resolutely in the three Tests, which the visitors shaded by very narrow margins'

O f the two 19th-century Test series described by some historians as the 'educational era' of South African rugby, the 1891 tour may well be regarded as the primary stage of the process, when the raw and eager South Africans were taught the finer points of the 'scientific game', as played in the mother country. The second venture, in 1896, was very much the secondary education, when many of the digested lessons of 1891 were implemented by the South Africans, with the fourth Test, the first ever won by South Africa, a kind of a graduation exam: South Africa had arrived on the world stage.

It was the then Western Province secretary, T.B. Herold, who was credited with the idea of inviting a team from the mother country to tour South Africa, and it was agreed by all concerned that such a tour would be of great benefit to South African rugby, then in its early stages of development. It was clear from the outset that if the tour to South Africa was going to go ahead, it

R. THOMPSON. T. WHITTAKER. E. MAYFIELD. W. WOTHERSPOON. A. ROTHERHAM. R. L. ASTON. C. P. SIMPSON. W. JACKSON.
W. E. BROMET. D. G. MacMILLAN. A. A. SURTEES. W. E. MACLAGAN. P. F. HANCOCK. W. G. MITCHELL. E. BROMET. J. H. GOULD
J HAMMOND. H. MARSHALL. P. R. CLAUSS.

was to be under the patronage of the Rugby Football Union, and not a private venture. The South Africans had offered guarantees for the tour expenses, but not until Sir Cecil Rhodes, the then prime minister of the Cape Colony, decided to underwrite the tour were the misgivings of the RFU secretary, the formidable George Rowland Hill, dissipated.

The next stage was the selection of a touring side of a reasonably high standard. The RFU-appointed selection committee, which included Hill, R.S. Whalley, H. Vassall, A. Budd and J.H.S McArthur, selected 21 players, many of whom were students at Oxford and Cambridge, under the captaincy of the legendary London Scottish and Scotland captain William E. 'Bill' Maclagan and managed by former Richmond and RFU secretary Edwin Ash. The tour would last some 60 days, with the tourists having to play 20 matches, including three Tests against the newborn rugby nation. Although only eight of the tourists were full internationals (four English, including Randolph Aston, and four Scottish, including Paul Clauss) and two more (Arthur Rotherham and Howard Marshall) won their caps after the tour, the party was considered very strong by all accounts.

Having left Southampton aboard the Dunottar Castle of the Castle Line on 20 June 1891, Bill Maclagan and his team – less Aubone Surtees, who travelled later – reached Cape Town in a record 16 days to be greeted with 'unlimited hospitality' by the locals. On 9 July 1891, three days after their arrival, the visitors took on the combined Cape Clubs in an historic first international match on African soil, in which they demonstrated their superior skill and pace against a reasonably strong side which included the captain of Western Province, Benjamin Duff, and three of the Versfeld brothers, one of whom, Charles 'Hasie' Versfeld, was the scorer of a try – the first and only South African score against the visitors throughout the 20-match tour.

ABOVE Bill Maclagan's 1891 team in South Africa. B.G. Roscoe and W.H. Thorman are missing from the photograph.

FACING PAGE A line out during the third Test at Cape Town.

The match referee was one of the most remarkable personalities of 19th-century South African rugby, Herbert Hayton 'H.H.' Castens, a player and coach with the Villagers club as well as manager and coach of the Western Province team. Two days later, on 11 July, Western Province, with Castens leading the forwards, gave the visitors a good run for their money but had to acknowledge defeat (6-0) to a better, faster and more knowledgeable side. Maclagan, who missed the second match, returned for the third against Cape Colony on the 13th, while the tireless Castens once again led the local forwards, who featured his younger brother Emile.

From Cape Town, the visitors travelled to Griqualand West for two matches, reaching Kimberley exhausted after a long journey by horse-drawn coach and train, yet with their enthusiasm and sense of adventure intact. Here they encountered very strong opposition but won both matches by 7-0 and 3-0 against Kimberley and Griqualand West respectively. The state of the field is described in the notes of Paul Clauss: '... we stepped into the arena with no little anxiety, as for the first time in our lives, we were going to play on a ground absolutely destitute of grass, hard and covered with reddish dust; so that, with a bright sun overhead, there was a considerable glare. Frequently, too, one lost sight of the ball in the pillars of dust that rose up in the wake of the players as they ran.'

From the red dust of Kimberley, Maclagan took his men to the lush, green lawns of Port Elizabeth for the next three matches, including the first ever Test played by South Africa. It was the former Scotland captain's return to international rugby after his retirement from it the previous season – an exciting prospect for one of the world's most capped players. The visitors had run riot against both Port Elizabeth Clubs (21-0) and Eastern Province (22-0), with the ubiquitous H.H. Castens, a native of Port Elizabeth, refereeing both encounters and his brother Emile playing for Eastern Province.

Indeed it was the 27-year-old H.H. Castens who was appointed the first ever captain of South Africa, although for reasons unknown he was not selected for the remaining two Tests. It is difficult to say whether it was his playing prowess that led to his downfall or the selection system in vogue in South Africa at the time, in which the provincial union hosting an international would select the team; or whether he simply opted out, having chosen to referee the final Test and the last match of the tour against Stellenbosch. His enormous role in the rapid evolution of the South African game from a raw battle of brawn to the combination of the scientific game as played in the British Isles cannot be overestimated. Even so, somehow a wicked strain of gossip reached posterity, suggesting that his selection to lead South Africa in their first Test had more to do with the influence of his father, Emilius Castens, in Eastern Province rugby than with his own ability.

In this respect a parallel between the playing careers of the two captains is instructive. Maclagan went to Scotland's leading rugby nursery, Edinburgh Academy, while Castens, six years younger, attended England's leading rugby establishment, Rugby School in Warwickshire. Both played cricket and rugby for their schools and both captained their school teams: Maclagan in 1874-75, Castens in 1882-83. Maclagan played back in the school 20-a-side team, then made his international debut in 1878 as the second sole full back in Scottish history, the game having changed from 20 players to 15 players a side. The following year he played in the first ever Calcutta Cup match against England and was described as 'one of the most powerful men behind the scrummage who have played for Scotland'. He was a ferocious tackler 'whose defence was not only sound, it was formidable' and 'a great master of the game'. He captained his country in six of the 26 internationals in which he played.

Castens, on the other hand, always played forward in 15-a-side rugby for school, university, club and country. In 1883, when Rugby School demolished Cambridge University by two goals and five tries to two goals and two tries, Castens, according to the school magazine, contributed 'splendidly throughout', as he tackled like a devil, scored tries, kicked at goal and led the forward rushes. That year he went up to Brasenose College, Oxford, winning his Blue in the 1886 Varsity Match. He played again for the university in 1887, which earned him an invitation to play for Middlesex County. Castens must have impressed the England selectors, since he was selected to play for the South of England against the North, a match organised to replace the missing fixtures against the three Celtic unions, who were boycotting England at the time. On his return to South Africa, the young law graduate joined the colonial administration and commenced playing for the Villagers club where, in the good tradition of Old Rugbeians, he became an inspiring and well-respected teacher and coach. Besides his exploits on the rugby field, Castens also went on to captain the South African cricket team on their maiden tour overseas in 1894, although they played no Tests on that trip.

Several years later, after Castens' death, his former rugby team-mate Barry Heatlie, a captain of South Africa, pointed out that 'we had the advantage of a great coach the late HH Castens, not long from Oxford University. Especially in regard to the forward play was it due to his tuition that we more than held the visiting pack.' Similarly Charlie van Renen, who like Heatlie played for South Africa against the

1891 tourists, pointed out that it was due to the coaching of H.H. Castens and Alf Richards that the playing standards of the Villagers club, of Western Province and ultimately of South Africa improved during the late 1880s and early 1890s. 'The solid foundation of our Rugby football was laid by Castens and Richards and subsequent development was largely due to their efforts,' he said.

Maclagan's men won all 20 matches on tour, although South Africa battled resolutely in the three Tests, which the visitors shaded by very narrow margins. Maclagan presented the gold cup received from Sir Donald Currie to the Kimberley team, in the opinion of the visitors the strongest of the 17 provincial teams they had encountered. Soon afterwards, the Griqualand West Rugby Football Union presented the cup to the South African Rugby Board, and as the Currie Cup it became the trophy for the interprovincial tournament and the holy grail of rugby football in South Africa.

Of the 1891 tour party, vice-captain Johnny Hammond, who returned to South Africa four years later with the 1896 team, R.G. MacMillan, Willie Mitchell and Randolph Aston played in every single one of the 20 matches, while Maclagan, Robert Thompson and William Bromet played in 19 of them. Aston was the top try scorer with an incredible tally of 30, with Edward Bromet and Maclagan a distant second and third with nine and eight respectively. In a speech, then SARB president Percy Ross Frames, who refereed four of the tour matches, including the second Test in Kimberley, expressed the hope that South Africa would benefit from the tour, which would enable them to send a strong team to Britain in the not so distant future. Fifteen years later, in 1906, Paul Roos' Springboks fulfilled this prophecy with a memorable tour of the British Isles.

OFFICIAL SPONSOR

The UK's No.1 South African wine brand

The taste of South Africa

INTERNATIONAL SCENE

Oh So Close
the 2009 Lions in South Africa

by **MICK CLEARY**

'The Lions had just six games to sort themselves out. They had to find a sense of themselves and of each other if they were to have any chance of making the series a contest'

We sent them on their way with a cheery wave, heartfelt best wishes and a grim realisation that it could all go horribly wrong. Much as their predecessors in 1997 had set out to do battle with South Africa, so Paul O'Connell's 2009 Lions headed south towards the end of May with it all to do to persuade people that not only could they compete with the world champions, they could beat them. Few believed that they could. Crucially, those with the faith included the most important men – management and players. If there were some players who didn't quite know what it was all about they would quickly get immersed in the culture of a Lions tour. All the more so one led by such Lions notables as Ian McGeechan and Gerald Davies. The pair were to be front of house throughout, men on the same wavelength, men with the core values of the Lions in their souls.

A Lions manager can sometimes be little more than an official functionary, there to press the flesh and protect the coach from intrusive outside matters, an important role but not fundamental to the success of the trip. Davies was different. He was there to bring the Lions back to a proper sense of themselves, to help inculcate those principles that had been swamped by the excesses of 2005. Back to basics; 'All for one and one for all' – call it what you will: Davies embodied that ethos.

It was McGeechan, of course, who had to put those values into practice out on the field of play. The Lions head coach knew that he had to get new-found team-mates onside with each other as quickly as possible; knew, too, that he had to get the players to really buy into the concept and not just spout platitudes at them. Players will only respond to guff for so long. Words had to mean something.

To that end, McGeechan had decided that first principles had to apply to everything. So there was to be only one coaching team for both midweek and Saturday sides. It had a familiar Wasps ring about it: Warren Gatland, Shaun Edwards and Rob Howley, with former Leicester and England prop Graham Rowntree backing up Gatland on forward duties. McGeechan's staff was first rate, from his medical people, headed by the indefatigable James Robson, through to his analysts, Rhys Long and Rhodri Bown. There were many others, all of whom did a splendid, selfless job. They weren't in it for acclaim, they were in it for each other. The squad would share rooms and travel together. Any hardship involved in being on the move so often would be overcome by that sense of it being a shared experience. Perhaps the modern pro had become too pampered, the game too po-faced and strait-laced. This lot were going to work hard and play hard. It was going to be fun.

McGeechan went for Paul O'Connell as captain, 2005 skipper Brian O'Driscoll being the only other contender. McGeechan believed in big, physical specimens for South Africa, and O'Connell fitted the bill. If O'Driscoll felt snubbed, it didn't show. Quite the opposite. O'Driscoll was relaxed and committed, a leader by example if not by title. He was to give the performance of a lifetime.

McGeechan chose a squad of 37, trimmed down significantly from Clive Woodward's approach four years earlier. Again, McGeechan believed that everyone had to have a fair crack at a Test place. For that to happen they had to have game time. The squad was a mix of senior pros such as Simon Shaw and Phil Vickery, interlaced with young thrusters such as Munster's Keith Earls and Cardiff Blues' Leigh Halfpenny, a man who was to come to know all about the slings and arrows of outrageous fortune. The real surprise was the inclusion of Munster flanker Alan Quinlan, who got the nod ahead of Leicester's Tom Croft. The arrangement was soon to change, Quinlan getting a 12-week ban for gouging. The Lions were also to lose Munster scrum half Tomás O'Leary, as well as hooker Jerry Flannery, both to injury. In all, ten players were to be sent home or fail to travel. The lot of the player in the big-hitting modern game is not an easy one.

The 2009 Lions were embarking on the shortest ever trip with the least amount of preparation time. If Munster had played Cardiff in the Heineken Cup final, then McGeechan would have been without 14 players for the training camp prior to departure. As it was, O'Driscoll and his Leinster chums, along with the downhearted, defeated Leicester duo of Croft and Harry Ellis, had barely 24 hours to get their kitbags packed before they were on their way south of the equator.

The Lions had just six games to sort themselves out. They had to find a sense of themselves and of each other if they were to have any chance of making the series a contest. It was no easy task. Winning the warm-up games was not the most important thing on McGeechan's agenda. He was prepared to sacrifice one or two of those if it meant that his team were able to hone part of their game in the process. You could see what McGeechan meant. But he also knew that trips such as these depend on momentum. Winning makes everything so much easier: self-belief is enhanced, training is more upbeat and players begin to trust not just in each other but also in the management.

The Lions just about managed to keep a clean sheet, winning all six lead-in games. But it was close. When they trailed 25-13 with only 14 minutes remaining of their opening game against the Royal XV in Rustenburg, the anxiety was beginning to show. But they held firm, scoring three tries through Lee Byrne, Alun-Wyn Jones and Ronan O'Gara, the Ireland fly half finishing with 22 points in the 37-25 victory.

BELOW Phil Vickery endures a torrid time against Tendai Mtawarira in the first Test.

FACING PAGE Celebrations for Rob Kearney's try as the Lions make a flying start in Pretoria.

The loosener was out of the way. It was time to get serious. The Lions responded in some style to that early stutter, seeing off the hapless Golden Lions 74-10 at Ellis Park. Already some things were beginning to take shape, notably a centre partnership of O'Driscoll and Jamie Roberts. The Lions experience was drawing the best from both,

the young Welshman growing in the exalted company. There was some lively play too from wing Tommy Bowe, Ugo Monye also, while Croft was beginning to show what an error it had been to omit him from the initial selection.

There was to be no evident divide between midweek and Saturday sides, between the traditional dirt-trackers and shadow Test team. In fact, it was the midweek line-up that played with more conviction. The Cheetahs came close in Bloemfontein, the Lions holding out for a 26-24 win. The midweek side then comfortably saw off the Sharks at Kings Park, 39-3. The final Saturday outing at a drenched Newlands required a late, nerveless long-range penalty goal from James Hook to preserve the unbeaten record, the Lions edging home 26-23 against Western Province.

The final warm-up game was a brutal affair in Port Elizabeth. The Southern Kings set out to rattle the teeth of the Lions just four days before the first Test, and they succeeded. There were high hits and cheap shots. The Lions lost two players in the 20-8 win, Hook to concussion and prop Euan Murray to a twisted ankle, an injury that was to rule him out of the tour. 'We knew there was going be some rough stuff on this tour and it came today,' said Gordon D'Arcy afterwards.

The Lions were just about intact and in good shape. McGeechan had promised that selection would go right to the wire. In reality, the Test players had revealed themselves. The truth of the matter was that one wing spot and one lock position were up for grabs. Monye got the left-wing berth while Alun-Wyn Jones got the nod to partner O'Connell. On form it was hard to disagree. Hooker Lee Mears had been the most accurate thrower to the line out, and the mobile Bath player also suited the intended game plan of trying to move around the big Springbok forwards.

The tension was rising as the Red Army descended on Durban. Once again, the Lions were proving a drawcard, the Kings Park stands packed with the red-shirted faithful. Attendances at the games had been below par, a result of a greedy ticket-pricing strategy rather than any lack of intrinsic interest. Whatever money did change hands for the three-Test series was not wasted. It was one of the finest series ever played, full of tension, edge, nerve, character and controversy.

There were so many unexpected shifts, beginning in Durban when the Lions scrum was taken apart. Poor Phil Vickery. The warrior figure on the Lions tight head was reduced to an impotent wreck by a combination of the scrummaging of Tendai 'the Beast' Mtawarira, slipshod refereeing

and a muted response from his own team-mates. Vickery's problems cost the Lions dear, both in terms of points on the board and of the momentum handed over to the Springboks. Vickery's transgressions, as he was obliged to dip and pop as the pressure came on, yielded nine points for South Africa through penalty kicks. New Zealand referee Bryce Lawrence was lenient on the Springbok binding and upward drive at the scrum.

In the old days the Lions would have sorted matters out in time-honoured '99' fashion. Instead they suffered in silence, putting up with it until Vickery was replaced by Adam Jones five minutes into the second half. By that stage the Springboks were 19-7 to the good, a lead they increased within two minutes of Jones coming on to the field, the Lions suffering the ignominy of being driven backwards from a line-out maul for Heinrich Brussow to touch down. Earlier John Smit had crashed through feeble defence, while the Lions had replied with a well-worked try through Croft.

At 26-7, the game appeared over. The Lions had different ideas, hitting the Springboks with everything they had. They played with real heart and intelligence, fully deserving their tries through Croft again and scrum half Mike Phillips. The Springboks were mightily relieved to win 26-21, and what might have been but for two gilt-edged missed opportunities by Monye preyed heavily on the minds of the crestfallen Lions fans as they headed out into the warm Durban night.

The Lions had to pick themselves up quickly. But how to do that when there was another game to play in Cape Town against the Emerging Springboks? There was to be no respite. The Lions were pegged back to a 13-13 draw at a storm-lashed Newlands and then had to prepare for a second Test at altitude at wet and windy sea level in Cape Town.

They overcame all those difficulties to give a tremendous account of themselves at Loftus Versfeld in Pretoria. They made five changes, Adam Jones and hooker Matthew Rees carrying on where they had left off in the front row, Rob Kearney coming in at full back, Luke Fitzgerald to the wing and, crucially, Simon Shaw to the second row. The Wasps lock finally started a Lions Test, 12 years and 17 games after first wearing the red shirt. He was outstanding in Pretoria as the Lions took the game to South Africa. They played with verve and confidence, racing to a 10-0 lead through a try from Kearney and kicks from Stephen Jones. True, they did concede a soft try to J.P. Pietersen from a set move at a line out, but they were in the ascendant. They would have cause to rue giving away a penalty on the stroke of half-time, landed by Frans Steyn, but they would have felt nothing but good about themselves as they went down the tunnel at the break with an 18-6 lead.

Calamity, though, was not far away. The Lions lost both props, Jones and Gethin Jenkins, within minutes of the restart and were obliged to go to uncontested scrums. Things got worse, the Lions losing both centres as well midway through the half. By then Bryan Habana had zipped past a groggy Brian O'Driscoll to close the deficit to four points at 19-15. Kicks were traded, Jaque Fourie smashed through weak tackling to touch down, and the scores eventually levelled at 25-25. Disaster was to strike Ronan O'Gara, though. With time almost up, the Irishman returned a kick to halfway and then gave away a reckless penalty by upending Fourie du Preez in the follow-up chase. Even then it was to take a heart-stopping 53-metre kick from replacement Morne Steyn, the very last act of a dramatic afternoon, to seal victory 28-25, and with it the series, for the Boks.

How different it all might have been if Schalk Burger's gouging of Fitzgerald had been seen clearly in the very first minute. Instead, the view of the officials was obscured, Burger was yellow-carded and the Boks escaped lightly. Burger was subsequently banned for eight weeks. The Burger affair did not die, particularly following crass comments by Springbok coach Peter de Villiers. The Lions were angry over that incident but devastated that the series had been lost. The margins may have been fine, but the reality was inescapable.

Both sides made wholesale changes for the third Test in Johannesburg. The Lions could have folded, but they were determined to go out on a high, to do justice to their generation. They did just that, posting a record-equalling score of 28-9. They would have bettered that mark but for the ball toppling off the kicking tee as Stephen Jones lined up the straightforward conversion of the first of Shane Williams' two tries. Monye, recalled to the colours, also got on the scoresheet, while there was a triumphant return to the side also for Vickery. It had been a memorable series of games. The Springboks got the spoils, but the Lions had an equal share of the plaudits.

Giving Something Back
50 Years of Penguin International
by ALAN WRIGHT

'In the past five years, no fewer than 600 men around the world have qualified as coaches through the HSBC/Penguin International Coaching Academy'

Penguin International RFC celebrated its first 50 years over the last weekend in May 2009 with a dinner at The Dorchester hotel and a special match played at Twickenham against The Commons & Lords RUFC, who by coincidence were celebrating their 25th anniversary. The match was played under Golden Oldies rules and the Penguin squad included several past internationals and distinguished players.

As its name suggests, the club has an international flavour. Its committee, chaired by Tom Wacker, past CEO of the IRB and currently a director of USA Rugby, is drawn from 15 nations, and Penguins have now coached and/or played in or against teams from a world record 62 countries/territories. In the abbreviated game, Penguins were recent semi-finalists at the Rome International Sevens and HSBC/COBRA International Tens in Malaysia, and won the Cup at the Eighth Borneo COBRA International Tens in Sandakan and the Plate at the Hong Kong International Tens. At home, besides their traditional annual fixtures against both Oxford and Cambridge Universities, during the course of their 50th year the club played anniversary matches to mark the centenary of Bedford Athletic RFC and the 125th anniversary of Sidcup RFC, of which club both Penguin founders were members.

An outstanding feature of the new millennium, though, has been the huge success and popularity of the HSBC/Penguin International Coaching Academy, ably directed by Craig Brown. In recent months the academy has carried out programmes in Borneo, China, Dubai, Guam, Hong Kong, Ireland and Malaysia. More recently still, and on behalf of the Asian Five Nations Committee, further programmes have been conducted in Jordan, Macau, Mongolia and Malaysia, where coaching was provided to the Indian and Pakistan national squads.

In the past five years, no fewer than 600 men around the world have qualified as coaches through the HSBC/Penguin International Coaching Academy. A special feature this year has been the invitation extended to the academy to coach in South Africa in association with the South African Rugby Union, HSBC and the British & Irish Lions. The Penguins, backed by HSBC, provided coaching support and organisation to the rugby festivals held during the Lions tour of South Africa, travelling the length and breadth of the country and helping to bring rugby to more than 1000 young children. Programmes were also conducted in seven cities, including a visit to Drakenstein Prison, Paarl, near Cape Town. One of the coaches on this occasion was Sai Nawavu, a popular instructor and past captain of Fiji, who has represented the Penguins in the Middlesex Sevens and on tour.

Penguin International is very proud to be sponsored by the great banking house, HSBC, the world's number one international bank, which has a network of some 10,000 offices in 83 countries and territories. HSBC was the principal partner of the British & Irish Lions tour to South Africa in 2009. The close association of Penguin International with HSBC has enabled it to follow an agreed policy of assisting the game to grow by nurturing interest at grass-roots level in communities worldwide.

Russia on the March
Will the Bears Make it to New Zealand?
by CHRIS THAU

'Under Diamond's hand the Russians have made further advances, reaching the runners-up berth in the 2008-10 Six Nations B, with valuable wins over Portugal and Romania'

ABOVE The Russian team pictured during the 2009 IRB Nations Cup in Bucharest.

One of the beneficial effects of the collapse of the Soviet Union has been the birth of a host of rugby nations, of which Georgia, Russia, Ukraine, Moldova, Latvia, Lithuania, Kazakhstan and Uzbekistan are, in that order, the most active and indeed successful. The Russians have invested substantial resources to change the pecking order at the top and replace Georgia as the most successful of the former Soviet republics. Under a new union president, Vyacheslav Kopiev, advised by former Sale chief executive Howard Thomas, they have employed former Sale and Saracens coach Steve Diamond as coach of the national team, with the specific objective of reaching the finals of the Rugby World Cup – an achievement that has eluded the Russians so far – in 2011.

Soviet rugby peaked during the late 1980s as the winds of Gorbachev's perestroika were playing havoc with the old structures of Soviet sport. During the 1980s, the Soviet Union became one of the leading nations of the Continental championship run by FIRA, managing to defeat Romania, Italy and even France A on a number of occasions. They toured England in 1989 and did well against England B in Northampton and returned for a full international against England in 1991. In recognition of the quality of their playing personnel, two of their former captains, Igor Mironov and Alexander Tikhonov, were elected Barbarians on the Baa-Baas' South Wales tour in 1990. However, by 1993 the Soviet Union was all but memory, and the structure of the once proud Soviet sporting machine in tatters.

Unlike Georgia, who embraced with great enthusiasm the opportunity to express themselves as a free and independent rugby nation, Russia – somehow reflecting the political ambiguity that followed the disintegration of the Soviet Union – failed to grasp the opportunities offered by the 'rugby revolution'. The break-up of the country into several independent republics, the economic crisis and the end of the state subsidies led to a reduction in the number of clubs from about 100 during the 1980s to 16 in 1993. The number reduced during subsequent years, the domestic scene stabilising at about 12 clubs and about 2000 players, of all ages, roughly divided between Siberia, the new centre of power of Russian rugby, and the Moscow region, with clubs also in Rostov and Chita. Unfortunately the 2000 miles between Moscow and the main centre of Siberian rugby, Krasnoyarsk, and the astronomic costs of domestic air travel have hampered the development of a truly nationwide competition, despite the regular exchanges between the two centres in the 11-strong club league.

The fall of communist dogma led to a decision of the newly formed Russian Rugby Federation to take part in the RWC 1995 qualifying rounds, having boycotted RWC 1991 for 'ideological' reasons. The first match of the newly born Russia was against Morocco in Moscow in March 1993, followed shortly by the RWC qualifying tournament in the town of Sopot in Poland. The Russians defeated both Georgia and Poland to qualify for the next round of qualifiers. During those years, the Russians had developed strong ties with Northern Transvaal, so after Sopot, the Russians toured southern Africa to prepare for the RWC 1995 qualifying tournament in Romania. In Bucharest their dreams of glory were short-lived as the Romanians, still a force to be reckoned with, inflicted the heaviest defeat in the short history of international exchanges between the two countries. The Russians failed again in their bid for the finals of RWC 1999, this time at the hands of Georgia, who derailed the Russian armoured train amid scenes of wild enthusiasm in Tbilisi.

The comparative success of their Sevens team, coached by South African Jim Stonehouse, in the finals of the RWC Sevens 2001 in Mar del Plata, when they defeated Georgia in the play-offs for seventh place, convinced the Russians to bite the bullet and appoint a foreign coach for the first time in their history. In March 2001, the Russians named former Western Transvaal and Cats coach James Stoffberg as national coach to help them qualify for RWC 2003. Stoffberg did reasonably well to add structure to the basically sound Russian playing pattern, but the language barrier and the hostility of the 'old guard' doomed his efforts. His tenure was brought to an end by defeat against their nemesis Georgia in the final rounds of the European qualifying process for RWC 2003, followed by the suspension of the Russians for using ineligible players in their Repechage matches against Spain.

In 2007 the trio of Romania, Portugal and Georgia managed to beat off the Russian challenge and reach the finals of the Rugby World Cup in France, but this did not deter the ambitious Russians, who went back to the drawing board. They appointed former Béziers flanker Claude Saurel as national coach, and he did well in his first year to take the team to the runners-up position in the 2006-08 European Nations Cup, popularly known as the Six Nations B. Previously Saurel had helped put Georgian rugby on the map after a reasonably successful stint with Morocco. He had also coached Tunisia to the finals of the RWC Sevens 2005, when the brave Tunisians did well to win a few matches, including one against the high-flying South Africans. The Russian Rugby Federation asked Saurel to concentrate on the Sevens team, who failed in their bid to win the European Championship. According to Moscow insiders, the failure of the Sevens team coupled with Russia's defeats in both their matches against Georgia in the Six Nations B may have weakened Saurel's position. However, it was Saurel himself who resigned defiantly when the Russians invaded Georgia, claiming in a widely publicised interview that he could not stand idle and watch as his friends in Tbilisi were bombed by the Russians.

This is when Diamond, a fiery former Sale hooker, appeared on the scene and was appointed technical director of the Russian Rugby Federation. His remit is quite extensive, including all development work, coach and referee training, age-group rugby and, of course, the national team. 'In my job I have to share my time between the national teams, age-group development and coaches' training, and I really relish it. But without a sound development framework in place, the

On day two it all took off, with a remarkable match right at the start of play involving England and Tunisia. England scored three quick tries to lead 19-0 and it looked all over. It wasn't. Tunisia hit back with a great try just before half-time to make it 19-7. From the kick-off at the start of the second half, England got their fourth try – 26-7 – and once again it looked all over. Once again, it wasn't. Tunisia, against all the odds, ran in three wonderful tries to close the gap to 26-24. Had they not missed two conversions, they could have produced one of the biggest upsets in the history of the World Cup Sevens.

That match was not the only surprise. In the topsy-turvy world of Sevens, little Portugal beat mighty Ireland 17-5. Who would have believed it? Argentina also caused a big ripple when they beat Wales 14-0 with a try in each half. Argentina were the better team and deserved to win. Little did we know these two sides would meet again in the final of the Cup competition the following day with a different result.

BELOW Martín Bustos Moyano crosses for the winning try for Argentina in their quarter-final against South Africa.

FACING PAGE Collins Injera scores for Kenya in their 26-7 quarter-final victory over Fiji.

PAGE 45 Aled Thomas wins the World Cup for Wales.

Nevertheless, all the fancied teams won their matches, and the eight sides that went through to the quarter-finals contained only one real surprise – Kenya. They lost 26-7 to England in their pool but beat Tunisia and Hong Kong, scoring 72 points, to finish as one of the best two runners-up and earn a quarter-final tie against Fiji.

The Bowl was a fascinating contest in its own right. It featured two teams from the Six Nations Championship (Ireland and Italy), the host nation (Arabian Gulf) and five further teams from the corners of the rugby world (Uruguay, Japan, Hong Kong, Georgia and Zimbabwe).

There were mixed fortunes in the quarter-finals for the Six Nations teams. The Irish had a big win over the Arabian Gulf, 24-5, but Italy lost 14-7 to Hong Kong. For their part, Zimbabwe racked up 28 points to Georgia's 10, while Uruguay edged home 19-12 against Japan. In the semi-finals Zimbabwe and Ireland had good wins over Uruguay and Hong Kong (24-7 and 22-15 respectively) to set up a cracking final. Zimbabwe raced to a half-time lead of 12-0. The Irish bounced back in the second half with two converted tries to take a 14-12 lead with just two minutes left. In a great finish, Zimbabwe scored the winning try in the very last minute to run out winners 17-14. Such a result could not have occurred in the 15-a-side game, but it did happen in Dubai in Sevens and was further proof if proof were needed that the smaller nations can match and beat the big guns in the abbreviated form of rugby.

The Plate competition went more or less to form. Tonga had no difficulty winning their quarter-final against Tunisia, scoring four first-half tries to lead at the interval 24-0, eventually triumphing 24-7. Australia beat the United States 24-14 and went on to reach the final with a narrow 22-19 victory over Tonga. In the bottom half of the draw, Scotland had a narrow but deserved 21-19 win over France, and Portugal defeated Canada 12-5. In their semi-final, Scotland cruised through against Portugal 29-7, running in five tries.

The Plate final was a tremendous match. Scotland got a try from the kick-off, but Australia hit back within two minutes with a converted try to draw level. On the stroke of half-time, Scotland scored a second try for an interval lead of 14-7. Midway through the second half, the Scots got a third try for what looked like a winning lead of 21-7, but the Wallabies ran in two unconverted tries in the last two minutes, and the Scots were very glad to hear the final whistle.

And so to the World Cup itself. A small but vociferous crowd gathered for the 12 pool matches on the first night of the competition, and these went as expected with the one exception of Scotland losing to heavily (33-14) to Canada. The four form teams and favourites for the Cup – Fiji, New Zealand, England and South Africa – all enjoyed comfortable wins. England and New Zealand each scored 42 points (42-5 v Hong Kong and 42-0 v Italy respectively), with Fiji and South Africa each running up a more conservative 26 points (26-10 v Georgia and 26-5 v Japan). No surprises there. Wales and Samoa, Kenya and Argentina also caught the eye with impressive performances.

The first Cup quarter-final on the last day of the tournament provided one of the closest and best matches of the entire three days. Wales faced the favourites New Zealand, and after just 59 seconds the Kiwis scored a converted try. The Welsh then dominated the rest of the first half, running in two great scores to put them 10-7 ahead. In the first minute of the second half, New Zealand broke through to score a second converted try to regain the lead 14-10. Wales never gave up, and in the final minute they scored their third try to snatch a dramatic victory – 15-14.

The second quarter-final was almost as exciting. Samoa outscored England by three tries to one in the first half and looked home and hosed, but England staged a brilliant recovery to level the match at 26-26 in added time at the end of the second half. In the sudden-death play-off, Samoa scored the winning try after two desperate minutes of attack and counterattack to triumph 31-26.

The third match was very close as well and involved an exciting comeback. South Africa led 12-0 five minutes into the second half, but then Argentina, with incredible bravado, launched two major attacks resulting in two tries, and with both converted they edged home 14-12. The last tie produced the only decisive result – against all expectations Kenya beat Fiji comprehensively 26-7, outscoring the 2005 World Cup holders by four tries to one.

The semi-finals both produced clear-cut winners. Wales defeated Samoa 19-12, while Argentina scored a try in each half to beat Kenya. However, full credit must be given to the Kenyans, who with a team full of sprinters and ball handlers had the whole crowd of 40,000 supporting them.

The final provided a fitting end to three great days of Sevens rugby. Wales led 12-7 – tries from Richie Pugh and Tal Selley and a conversion from Aled Thomas against a try and conversion from Martín Rodríguez. Gonzalo Camacho then scored a second try for Argentina to bring the scores level at 12-12, but with time running out Aled Thomas scored the winning try for Wales. He added the conversion and the celebrations began.

It had been an amazing day's rugby. The four favourites had all lost in the quarter-finals, whereas Wales and Argentina – both rank outsiders at the start of the tournament – deserved all credit for scaling the heights and producing a great final. There have now been four different winners of the Sevens World Cup – England, Fiji (twice), New Zealand and Wales – just as there have been four different winners of the 15-a-side World Cup – New Zealand, Australia (twice), South Africa (twice) and England. The first ever double Rugby World Cup Sevens – men's and women's – was a big success. Let us hope this formula is continued, and above all let us hope the members of the IOC report back after their fact-finding mission to recommend that Sevens be included in the 2016 Olympics.

Women's RWC Sevens

by REBECCA BUTLER

'The match went into extra-time sudden death. Australia were soon awarded a penalty and Matcham scored in the corner to clinch victory and create history'

History was made earlier this year as the first ever Women's Sevens World Cup took place alongside the men's tournament in Dubai. Women's Sevens is still an amateur sport and very much still in its infancy. However, prior to the World Cup, the players had already proved their skill, their commitment to the game and their fiercely physical competitiveness in the high standard of the international Sevens circuit. The women raised the bar at the inaugural Women's World Cup and gave the spectators a brilliant tournament.

The first day of pool games saw a huge number of tries and some hotly contested matches. Australia's Tricia Brown and Bo De la Cruz both scored hat-tricks in their opening game against China (50-12), and France had an epic match to come from behind to also beat China 19-5. In Pool B, top seeds England gave fantastic performances to book their place in the Cup quarter-finals against strong second seeds Australia. Captain Sue Day inspired her team-mates with two tries in their opening match against USA (17-0), and England went on to complete the day without conceding a point.

Spain took control of Pool C from the start with a 19-0 victory over Brazil and went on to secure their place in the third Cup quarter-final. Canada got the chance to shine on Pitch 1, and a hat-trick

ABOVE The Australian Women's Sevens team are crowned world champions after winning the inaugural Women's RWC Sevens.

PAGE 50 Shelly Matcham dives in for the winning score against New Zealand in the final.

Hong Kong: One Glorious Weekend

by IAN ROBERTSON

'Can I pick just one moment to highlight the ethos of the Cathay Pacific Sevens? Yes. At 1.40 on Sunday afternoon, Kenya produced a moment of magic'

March was an interesting month for the game of Sevens. First there was the World Cup (RWC Sevens) in Dubai and then three weeks later the legendary Cathay Pacific Sevens in Hong Kong, which I have been devoted to for the past 29 years.

Both were great tournaments, but I have to conclude that Hong Kong leaves every other Sevens competition in the world in its wake. It has the very best atmosphere in the very best stadium with the very best players performing in front of the very best spectators. It simply doesn't come any better than that and 2009 was every bit as good and as much fun as ever.

It all boils down to the fact that Hong Kong became the first place in the world to regularly host a great Sevens tournament annually in front of a huge audience. Initially in the early 1980s it took place in front of several thousand fans and then ever since in front of a sell-out crowd of 40,000, year after year. It's all about the South Stand, the bonhomie, the fun, the family atmosphere, the beat of the music, the fans, the sponsors and of course the quality of the rugby. It is about all that is best in rugby coming together for one glorious weekend once a year on the vibrant island of Hong Kong.

RIGHT Kenya do it again. Having beaten Fiji in Dubai, the East Africans conquered New Zealand in Hong Kong.

FACING PAGE A merry dance. Emosi Vucago of Fiji leaves a trail of South African defenders during the final of the Cup.

Can I pick just one moment to highlight the ethos of the Cathay Pacific Sevens? Yes. At 1.40 on Sunday afternoon, Kenya produced a moment of magic as they trailed New Zealand. In the first half Zar Lawrence had scored a try for the Kiwis straight from the kick-off. Tomasi Cama converted – 7-0 to New Zealand. Four minutes later, Innocent Simiyu sprinted clear to score a try for Kenya. Unconverted – 7-5 to New Zealand. Then in the middle of the second half, Simiyu ran in his second try to put Kenya 10-7 ahead. The moment of magic brought the whole stadium to its feet. Forty thousand fans went ballistic. The South Stand exploded, the music blared out and the crowd threw a massive comfort blanket round the Kenyan team, which inspired them to defend, cover and tackle for five frantic minutes – and against all the odds and the weight of history, they held on to beat New Zealand. It was a triumph to savour. It proved the impossible is always possible. That was my ultimate memory of a wonderful weekend.

The Bowl competition produced more than the usual number of one-sided matches. All four quarter-finals were won decisively, with Japan, Portugal, Uruguay and Zimbabwe cruising through to the last four. In the semi-finals, Portugal outscored Japan by four tries to two (26-10), and Uruguay had a comfortable 28-14 win over Zimbabwe.

In the final we enjoyed the best and closest match of the Bowl. João Mirra scored the only try of the first half to give Portugal a 7-0 lead. Midway through the second half, Frederico Oliveira scored a second try for Portugal, and with Pedro Leal's conversion the 14-0 lead looked conclusive. But in the final two minutes, Uruguay hit back with two tries from Ignacio Conti and Santiago Carracedo. Sadly for the South Americans, Nicolás Morales only converted one, which left Portugal the 14-12 winners of the Bowl.

The Plate competition featured three teams from the Six Nations Championship, but that counted for nothing as France, Wales and Scotland all failed to reach the final. The big disappointments were Wales. They had hit the heights to win the World Cup Sevens in Dubai three weeks earlier, but only two of that team were available for the Cathay Pacific Sevens, and after struggling to beat the USA 22-21 in the Plate quarter-final, they lost 19-10 to Canada in the semis. In the other half of the draw, Scotland were eclipsed 29-0 by Tonga, whilst France reached the semi-finals with a 17-7 victory over Korea. Tonga then progessed to the final with a 19-10 win over France.

Just like that of the Bowl, the Plate final was a desperately close game. D.T.H. van der Merwe and Sean Duke scored tries for Canada, which with one converted led to a 12-7 Canadian advantage at half-time, Peasipa Moimoi having scored and converted a Tongan try just before the break. In a dramatic climax, in the very last move of the match Nili Latu crossed to level the scores. Moimoi added the conversion to leave Tonga 14-12 winners of the Plate.

The Cup competition on the final day produced four very closely contested quarter-finals, including the biggest shock of the whole weekend. As mentioned earlier, when little-fancied Kenya beat tournament favourites New Zealand by 10 points to 7 it was hugely emotional to hear the full house of 40,000 supporters screaming their approval. It was a truly remarkable one-off result which set tongues wagging, hands clapping and feet stamping in a wonderful standing ovation for the Kenyan team.

Not surprisingly, their heroic defensive effort in tackling themselves and the New Zealanders to a standstill took its toll and they lost to Fiji in the semi-finals, albeit only by 24 points to 7. Earlier, Fiji had had to work very hard in their quarter-final, edging past England 10-7. Fiji scored first through Pio Tuwai to go 5-0 ahead at half-time. England took the lead three minutes into the second half with a try by Rob Vickerman, converted by Ben Gollings – 7-5. But in a thrilling finish, Fiji scored the winning try from Emosi Vucago with the very last move of the game. England had been shell-shocked to lose in the quarter-finals of the World Cup Sevens in Dubai and were now devastated at their failure to reach the semi-finals in Hong Kong.

In the top half of the draw, South Africa outscored Australia by four tries to two (24-10) to earn a semi-final tie against Samoa, who beat Argentina 15-12 in the quarter-finals with the very last kick of the game – a penalty by Lolo Lui. The latter was a tremendous game, with the Samoans leading

12-5 at half-time and Argentina drawing level in the opening minute of the second half. It stayed at 12-12 until that winning penalty. Samoa had shot their bolt, though. They had nothing left in the semi-finals and lost to South Africa 29-3.

The final proved to be the perfect end to three perfect days of all that is best in Sevens rugby. Fiji were installed as favourites and it looked all over after seven minutes of the first half when they led 19-0 with two tries from Emosi Vucago and another from Osea Kolinisau plus two conversions from Vucago. However, South Africa are nothing if not competitive. Before half-time they staged a full-blooded recovery, with a try each from Renfred Dazel and Robert Ebersohn. Dazel added a conversion to leave Fiji in front at the interval by 19 points to 12.

Three minutes into the second half, Fiji looked to have wrapped up the match with a converted try by Seremaia Burotu – 26-12 to Fiji. Not a bit of it. South Africa's Vuyo Zangqa burst through to score, then kicked the conversion – 26-19 and all to play for. In the third minute of added time, the Fijian defence was prised open and Lionel Mapoe crashed over – 26-24 to Fiji with the South African conversion from way out near the touch line to come. Mzwandile Stick narrowly failed to grab his 15 seconds of glory, and the final whistle went to leave Fiji the winners of the Cup.

It was, as ever, a brilliant three days of competition, and full credit to Cathay Pacific in particular, who have sponsored this tournament as far back as I can remember. The Hong Kong Rugby Union also deserve a big pat on the back for their ruthlessly efficient administration. Once again, the Cathay Pacific Sevens confirmed its status as the best Sevens tournament in the world.

The World Cup Sevens in Dubai were good. The Hong Kong Sevens were just so much better. Both were great adverts for the International Olympic Committee to include rugby Sevens in the 2016 Olympics. The omens are very encouraging.

Reach the modern heart of China with Cathay Pacific.

...agonair, we offer more flights from

...e warmth of Asian hospitality from the moment

...thaypacific.co.uk or contact your travel agent.

future Brumbies team-mates Stephen Hoiles and Patrick Phibbs. On leaving school in 2000, he signed with the National Rugby League's Sydney Roosters. Mackay played five seasons with the Roosters' SG Ball (Under 18), Jersey Flegg (Under 21) and Premier Division sides before going back to rugby union in 2004.

His return signalled the beginning of an extensive Sevens career from 2004 to 2008, which included taking over captaincy of the Australian Sevens side from 2005. His team-mates talk of him leading from the front; he was more about action than words. A career highlight was skippering a team laced with Wallabies at the 2006 Commonwealth Games in Melbourne.

That same year, 2006, Mackay signed with the Waratahs, earning six state caps for the New South Wales side in the Australian Provincial Championship and on the end-of-season development tour of the United Kingdom and Ireland. In 2007, he joined the Melbourne Rebels for the Australian

FACING PAGE South Africa's Ryan Kankowski cannot stop Macca scoring as Australia win 20-14 in the quarter-finals at the Melbourne Commonwealth Games.

RIGHT Shawn is lifted during a line-out drill at a Brumbies training session in Durban ahead of the Super 14 match against the Sharks in March 2009.

Rugby Championship, the side making the competition final.

Meanwhile, at club level, after four years representing Randwick in Sydney's club competition, Mackay moved to the University of Queensland club in Brisbane on completion of the 2008 Sevens calendar, with a view to staking his claim for selection in the Queensland Reds Super 14 squad. Despite University's lowly finish to the season, Mackay was selected in the representative Queensland XV that defeated Air New Zealand Cup side Auckland 42-0 in June and signed with the Brumbies the following month.

Mackay was known for his uncompromising defence and polished ball skills, and he scored many tries throughout his distinguished Sevens and club rugby career. However, besides being a fine player, Mackay also enjoyed success as a coach. In 2008 he coached the first-ever Australian Women's Sevens side to the Oceania Sevens title – they were unbeaten in the competition – and automatic qualification for the inaugural Rugby World Cup Sevens women's event in Dubai in March 2009. Just a month before Shawn passed away, Australia went on to become the Women's Rugby World Cup Sevens champions by defeating New Zealand in extra time. The Wallaroos, who shared Mackay's

gusto and 'can-do' approach, said they would forever remember him as 'one of the girls'. Taking on the coaching role with the Wallaroos said a lot about Shawn: evidence of his passion for rugby and eagerness to be involved and to contribute in every way he could.

More than a thousand mourners gathered for Shawn Mackay's farewell at Waverley's Mary Immaculate Church in Sydney's eastern suburbs. It was fitting that Morgan Turinui and Shawn's younger brother Matt should lead the pall-bearers, who carried Mackay's coffin to the hearse as Elton John's *Don't Let The Sun Go Down On Me* played. The coffin was then driven through a 300-metre tunnel of past and present team-mates. In keeping with Shawn's personality, everyone who had filled the church to capacity for the service, or had stood outside to listen to it broadcast through speakers, broke into applause.

Many former and current players and officials from both codes attended the service. Mackay's Brumbies team-mates travelled up to Sydney from Canberra; Waratah players with whom he competed in six games in 2006 attended; and some even came from the Western Force. Australian Sevens players flew in from around the country, and there were past and present rugby league players from the Roosters, with whom he won a Jersey Flegg title. Mackay's footy ties were recognised with the placement on his coffin of the jerseys he wore – from Clovelly Eagles, through Waverley College, to the Roosters, Randwick, Melbourne Rebels, Australian Sevens and the Brumbies.

The Mackay family was touched by the outpouring of grief and praise for Shawn. His parents, John and Leonie, said their son would have been 'humbled' by the tributes to him from the grass roots through to international rugby. Shawn's uncle and godfather, John Hurley, said in his eulogy: 'We are only just realising what an impact he had on so many people.' He added: 'As we all know, rugby is the game they play in heaven and we know who will be the captain of the side.'

From Turinui to Matt Mackay, Hurley and even the priests at the funeral – all spoke of Shawn's incredible zest for life. They remembered him placing his first bet as a five year-old – '50 cents on the nose', said Hurley. Turinui recalled Shawn's two favourite horses were *Sunline*, because it led from the start, and *Octagonal*, for the way it got out of impossible situations to win. He also spoke of Macca winning the prestigious CAS (Combined Associated Schools) 800m and 1500m athletics titles and becoming known as the 'White Kenyan'.

As Father Lucas so appropriately commented: 'He might not have had a full life, but it sounds to me he was full of life.' And he was.

Shawn Mackay will be missed by his parents, John and Leonie, younger brother Matt, sister Kristy and partner Trish Scott, as well as by countless others throughout the Australian rugby community. May he rest in peace.

FACING PAGE Mourners gather outside Waverley's Mary Immaculate Church to say farewell to Shawn Mackay.

BELOW Shawn Mackay (third from left, back row) with the Australian Seven that won the Plate at the inaugural Adelaide Sevens in 2007. They beat South Africa 31-0 in the final.

Blacks Unchallenged
the 2009 Junior World Championship
by ALAN LORIMER

'It had been another glorious exhibition from the young All Blacks and a chance to watch future New Zealand senior players in action. Top among these future stars was Aaron Cruden'

They may have fallen short of expectations in certain global competitions but New Zealand continue to be the most successful rugby nation in age-grade rugby after adding the 2009 IRB Junior World Championship title to their extensive list of age-group achievements. The Baby Blacks, unchallenged as yet in the Under 20 age group, set incredible standards throughout the tournament, demonstrating to the crowds in Japan and to a global television audience that rugby union is a game of subtle running and passing skills rather than brute physical force.

This was only the second world championship at Under 20 level, a conflation of the previous Under 19 and Under 21 global tournaments, but already changes have been announced for future competitions. As from next year there will be a reduction in the number of teams from 16 to 12, the idea being to make the tournament less expensive and easier to administer for the host country.

Not that the 2009 championship hosts, Japan, were constrained by either of these considerations. At the end of a successful championship, Japan, originally touted as possible contenders to stage the 2011 Rugby World Cup, proved themselves able to put on a global rugby event. If there were shortcomings, they were to do with the decision to stage the pool matches in the four major cities

of the country – Tokyo, Osaka, Nagoya and Fukuoka. It meant that it was not possible to follow more than one pool, thus creating a sense of disconnection within the tournament. One further problem was the climate – both heat and humidity – which posed difficulties for the players.

The announcement of the coming change in the number of participating teams was made just before the tournament started, with the advice that only the top 12 would qualify for the 2010 championship, or the top 11 if next year's hosts, Argentina, finished in the bottom four. While this situation was seen by the big fish as being of little consequence, it had a mind-concentrating effect on the lower teams. In the event Japan and Uruguay, both fourth seeds in their pools, and two third seeds in Canada and Italy made up the bottom four and thus will not be competing in the 2010 tournament. Fiji and Tonga, meanwhile, each finished third in their pools to ensure survival in the competition, much to the delight of the IRB, who have poured oceans of money and resources into rugby development in these countries. Their strong showing also gave a boost to Pacific Island rugby and projected the possibility of their becoming strong rugby sides in their own right at senior level rather than feeders for New Zealand and Australia.

It seemed that this might be the year for a northern hemisphere side to break through as France had done at Under 21 level in 2006, when they defeated South Africa. England carried European hopes after finishing runners-up in the 2008 final, but a question mark hung over their chances after losses to Ireland and France in the Under 20 Six Nations Championship. The England team, drawn almost wholly from Premiership clubs,

LEFT New Zealand celebrate after securing the IRB Junior World Championship once again, having beaten England in the final for the second year in succession.

looked impressive at the Prince Chichibu Stadium in Tokyo as they put 43 points past a Japan side that certainly did not lack skill or courage. Scotland offered a lot more resistance but eventually succumbed 30-7 in round two of the pool matches. Then in their final pool game England produced brilliant form to record a 52-7 win against Samoa to top their group and gain a place in the semi-finals against South Africa. The Baby Boks had eased past Fiji 36-10 before securing an easy 65-3 win against Italy, but in their last pool match they had to work hard to defeat France 43-27 in the heat of Osaka.

South Africa had ambitions to improve on their third-place finish in last year's tournament in Wales, but it was not to be. England, after trailing 9-11 at the break, made their forward strength tell in the second half – helped by the red card shown to South Africa flanker Rynhardt Elstadt – to win comfortably 40-21, with tries from Ben Youngs, James Gaskell and Henry Trinder.

New Zealand, meanwhile, had swept through their pool with victories over Uruguay (75-0), Ireland (17-0) and Argentina (48-9) on their way to an expected group victory in Nagoya and a semi-final against Australia. The 7-7 scoreline at half-time in that semi-final demonstrated the closeness of these two rivals, but in the second half New Zealand showed their prowess to run in three tries for a 31-17 victory and a place in the final against England.

In steamy conditions at the Prince Chichibu Stadium, New Zealand virtually made certain of retaining their title with a brilliant first-half performance that produced four tries, two from fly half Aaron Cruden and one apiece from full back Robbie Robinson and winger Zac Guildford. England replied with a try from lock James Gaskell and three penalty goals from London Irish full back Tom Homer. New Zealand were able to add three further tries in the second half, from centre Shaun Treeby, Guildford and hooker Brayden Mitchell, to clinch the match, despite a better second-half showing from England, who scored through No. 8 Carl Fearns and replacement scrum half Dave Lewis.

It had been another glorious exhibition from the young All Blacks and a chance to watch future New Zealand senior players in action. Top among these future stars was Aaron Cruden, who was rightly voted the IRB Junior Player of the Year. His achievement was all the more remarkable in that he overcame testicular cancer a few months earlier. Little wonder that his sporting hero is Lance Armstrong. Cruden was simply a maestro on the pitch, having the full repertoire of skills and the kind of rugby brain that puts him ahead of everyone else. Watch out for this name in the near future.

Cruden, of course, benefited from having other hugely talented players in the New Zealand team, of whom Brayden Mitchell will surely climb the ladder, along with centre Winston Stanley (nephew of the great Joe Stanley), Robbie Robinson and Zac Guildford, who tragically suffered bereavement with the death of his father at the final.

England, too, revealed stars of the future. Sale's Carl Fearns, impressive throughout the tournament, was nominated for the Junior Player of the Year award. Yet Fearns was only one of a clutch of exciting English players to catch the eye, top among them centres Luke Eves and Henry Trinder, Tom Homer and James Gaskell.

Australia's stand-out player was undoubtedly Richard Kingi. The live-wire scrum half opened up defences with his scorching breaks and he looks certain to appear in a senior Wallaby shirt. Kingi was on the bench for the first half of Australia's third-place play-off against South Africa, and his

absence seemed palpable as the Baby Boks established a winning 18-5 position at the break, with two converted tries in the second half making the final score 32-5. Another half back to dazzle was fly half Pierre Bernard, whose 33 points contributed to France's 68-13 victory over a disappointing Wales in the fifth-place play-off. Meanwhile, Samoa edged out Ireland in the seventh-place play-off with a 9-3 win in an uninspiring game.

The remaining Celtic nation, Scotland, found themselves in the third-tier (ninth-to-twelfth-place) group after being hit by an injury-time dropped goal that gave Samoa a 17-14 victory in their pool match. A draw would have been sufficient for Scotland to qualify for the fifth-to-eighth-place group, and having achieved wins over both Wales and Ireland in the Six Nations the Scots felt that this was their level. Scotland, however, showed their mettle with subsequent wins over Fiji (39-26) and Tonga (28-25) to take ninth place, while Argentina, whose form had been below par, rallied to defeat Fiji 27-10 for eleventh place. In the last group of four, Italy recovered some ground by beating Canada 32-22 for thirteenth place, while hosts Japan delighted the home support with a 54-17 win over Uruguay to take fifteenth place.

Overall standards continue to rise, but there is now a growing divide between the countries who can field professional players and those whose unions cannot afford this luxury. The 2010 tournament in Argentina will undoubtedly reflect this fissure, but that should not detract from what could potentially be a more exciting tournament. Roll on Rosario!

BELOW Fly half Andrew White is collared during Scotland's 12-7 pool victory over Japan at Tokyo's Prince Chichibu Stadium.

Summer Tours 2009
England v Argentina

by CHRIS FOY

'Delon Armitage's exploits served to once again make a mockery of the Lions coaches' decision to exclude him from the squad in South Africa'

As a sad sign of the times, financial necessity served to dilute one of the most exotic and taxing assignments in world rugby. What was meant to be a 'tour' of Argentina, instead became akin to a European football-style home-and-away tie. In the circumstances, England weren't complaining. A fortnight in the Pumas' famously inhospitable domain at the end of a shattering season, without nine leading players who were in South Africa with the Lions, would have been a daunting expedition. So when the Argentine rugby union (UAR) approached their counterparts at the RFU to ask for the first of two Tests in the series to be played in England, it was an easy decision to answer in the affirmative. By doing so, officials at Twickenham were able to reveal a caring, sharing sense of the bigger picture by allowing all gate receipts – some £500,000 – to be transferred to Buenos Aires, to assist the hard-up UAR. It also meant they could spare national manager Martin Johnson and his depleted squad the onerous task of enduring back-to-back matches in Argentina, where more accomplished teams than the current Red Rose vintage have come unstuck. And finally, it allowed them to indulge in a spot of missionary work, by hosting the first of the two Tests at Old Trafford in an attempt to expand union's supporter base in the northwest.

Yet, while the administrators had created a rugby version of a two-legged UEFA Cup fixture, the same criteria didn't apply to declaring a winner when the series ended all square at 1-1. If it had been decided on aggregate scores, England would have prevailed comfortably – 59-39. Johnson's side would have also been the victors if it had come down to 'away tries', courtesy of Matt Banahan's last-minute effort in the second match in Salta. As it was, the Pumas were able to wave a trophy around for the benefit of their raucous supporters, by virtue of having won the previous encounter between the two nations, at Twickenham in November 2006. Argentina's need for success was perhaps greater than England's anyway, as prior to this series they had won just two of their seven Tests since memorably finishing third at the 2007 World Cup.

The encounter in Manchester on 6 June was a damp squib on a typically damp day, yet Johnson's face radiated sunny satisfaction after watching his men grind the 'home' side down, to win 37-15. There were 22 points from the boot of fly half Andy Goode – four penalties,

BELOW Andy Goode kicks one of his two dropped goals in the first Test at Old Trafford.

FACING PAGE Delon Armitage chips through to set up Matt Banahan's try in the first Test.

PAGE 71 Matt Banahan goes past Francisco Leonelli to score in the second Test at Salta.

two conversions and two dropped goals – as England went about their work in pragmatic fashion. It was like watching old-school Leicester at Welford Road. No wonder the manager loved it.

Although the crowd of 40,000 savoured the first-hand experience of an England victory, they were not impressed by the dearth of running rugby and made their feelings known with boos and jeers. Remarkably, given the limited scope of their attacking play, England did actually manage to score three tries, but it was perhaps no surprise that they all stemmed from kicks.

The first came from Banahan, who had already touched down on his senior international debut against the Barbarians at Twickenham a week earlier. The fact that he scored again in Salta meant the giant Bath wing had a return of three tries from his first three England appearances. More than that, he made a significant impression on Johnson with his commitment and desire to learn. The former lock from Jersey has the physique to terrorise defences, as he showed in mowing down an opponent en route to the line in the second Test. He also has a handy knack of appearing in the right place at the right time, and in addition to having an inquisitive mind, he is a genial, outgoing character, making him an ideal tourist. In short, Banahan was a real find.

There was another of those in the equally robust shape of David Wilson, the young tight-head who moved from Newcastle to Bath after this series. Having acquitted himself well against a formidable Barbarians pack in the match before the encounter in Manchester, he gave an accomplished scrummaging performance against the Argentina forwards, whose set-piece prowess is the stuff of legend.

England's other try scorer at Old Trafford was Delon Armitage, who crossed twice. Bizarrely, he was set up on both occasions by instinctive volleys from Mark Cueto, but the London Irish full back had the poacher's instinct to pounce on those unexpected opportunities. His exploits served to once again make a mockery of the Lions coaches' decision to exclude him from the squad in South Africa, despite a torrent of early-tour injuries leaving the door wide open for a call-up. With trademark understatement, Johnson expressed his surprise that Armitage remained at his disposal, and that view was further enhanced a week later when it was the No. 15's sublime backhand offload that sent Banahan galloping away to score.

Argentina chose to take the second Test to the northwest of their country, to the picture-postcard lower slopes of the Andes, close to the border with Chile. Against this glorious backdrop, the Pumas

LEFT Salta, second Test. Juan Manuel Leguizamón, scorer of the first Puma try, is held up this time by England skipper Steve Borthwick, aided by flanker Chris Robshaw (No. 6).

were very different beasts in front of their own public, having gone down without much of a fight in Manchester. Flanker Juan Manuel Leguizamón scored an early try from a loose England line out to set the scene for a rampaging performance which inspired his side. While the hosts still probed in narrow channels and relied on the assured kicking of their stand-off, Juan Martín Hernández, they operated at a far higher intensity than at Old Trafford, and England were unable to stand their ground in the eye of the storm.

There was one especially chastening moment for Johnson and his defence coach, Mike Ford, to endure. Just after half-time, Horacio Agulla was allowed to sail serenely through the centre unchallenged and he duly sent Gonzalo Camacho clear to touch down on the left. England's midfield defence had been alarmingly exposed in the Barbarians match, and here was another horrific lapse – not what Ford needed to send him into the close season.

Yet, amid the disappointment of a 24-22 defeat after three successive Test victories, there were positive elements to fall back on. Goode again delivered a fine goal-kicking performance under pressure, and Banahan maintained his ducks-to-water introduction to the international arena. There was also further evidence that hooker Dylan Hartley had learned to control his temper while not diminishing his aggressive, confrontational style. With Cueto reasserting his international credentials and Steffon Armitage firmly banishing grim memories of his debut against Italy back in February, there were encouraging signs that Johnson had increasingly deep resources to call upon. Yet, the manager only deals in the bottom line – victories, however they come – so the fact that England lost two of their three end-of-season matches will have tainted his overall sense of optimism.

Wales in North America

by GRAHAM CLUTTON

'Whilst the form of some senior players was outstanding, the emergence of Biggar, Davies, Daniel Evans, Jonathan Spratt and Sam Warburton provided the bigger smile'

A lthough the eyes of the world were on South Africa, where the British & Irish Lions were doing battle with the Springboks, Welsh rugby's focus fell on North America, where coach Robin McBryde led a relatively inexperienced Wales squad to victories over the USA and Canada. Forced into serious alterations in personnel but obviously excited at the opportunity to blood a handful of new faces, McBryde utilised his party well as the host nations were successfully put to the sword on successive weekends.

ABOVE Tom James takes on Canada's Sean Duke on his way to the line to score Wales's second try in their 32-23 victory in Toronto.

Furthermore, when the dust began to settle on this particular excursion across the pond, McBryde was understandably pleased with the collective effort and individual development of players like Dan Biggar, Tom James, Jonathan Davies and the returning Chris Czekaj. With Lee Byrne, Jamie Roberts, Shane Williams, Stephen Jones, Mike Phillips and Alun-Wyn Jones amongst those on duty for the

Lions, McBryde spent the final weeks of last season piecing together a squad that would not only come home unbeaten but would provide Warren Gatland with greater strength in depth ahead of the upcoming games in the autumn series.

Whilst the form of senior players Dafydd Jones, Mark Jones and Gareth Cooper was outstanding, the emergence of Biggar, Davies, Daniel Evans, Jonathan Spratt and Sam Warburton provided the bigger smile. 'To a man I think they made an enormous impression,' said McBryde. 'They certainly showed there is some strength in depth in Wales.

'Obviously there was a little bit of disappointment that we didn't manage to finish the job off properly against the Canadians and reach the standard of performance we were hoping to get. However, we had a number of youngsters out there on the day and they would have benefited greatly from the experience.'

With Martyn Williams likely to hang up his international boots this season, the form of Warburton in the second Test was certainly significant, whilst the difficulties surrounding Gavin Henson and the ongoing injury problems of Tom Shanklin mean Davies too could spring to the fore in the autumn after his try-scoring exploits. The young Scarlet showed power and pace against the Eagles, and on the back of a full season with his region looks bang on target to make the ultimate step. Biggar, too, has matured into a prolific outside half, whilst Evans and Spratt are two more who have earned a place in the possibles list, at least.

McBryde hinted that the regions might have a few selection issues with some of the younger players pushing to start for their sides. He said, 'Next season will be interesting. The younger players have shown they are good enough and that they need a bit more experience and a bit more exposure. We are in discussions with the regions. A good example is someone like [prop] John Yapp who we wanted to give time on the tight-head. The Blues have given him a little bit of game-time there and it's hugely beneficial to them to have him playing loose and tight. For us as a national squad as well it's good for us he is playing loose and tight.'

As for the youngest members, like Evans, Biggar and Craig Mitchell, McBryde added, 'They have had a good opportunity on the tour. They have had a taste of international rugby and hopefully that will spur them on to train a bit harder and want to win the shirt at regional level. After that, who knows?'

Biggar's boot proved the difference as Wales had to overcome stubborn resistance before defeating Canada 32-23 at York Stadium in Toronto. The Ospreys teenager, who made his senior international debut last season, collected 22 points and impressed with his all-round game, whilst Jonathan Davies also stood out on his debut. Czekaj, too, winning his first cap since breaking his leg in Brisbane two years previously, looked a potent force as he crossed for a popular try in the first half. Biggar's conversion of Czekaj's try and two successful penalties gave Wales a handy 13-6 lead inside the opening 25 minutes, and though Canada caught the Welsh defence napping in the 59th minute, when captain Pat Riordan sent in Ed Fairhurst for a try, Biggar made sure of victory with a late penalty.

Seven days later, the USA Eagles had their wings firmly clipped by a businesslike Wales side who ran out 48-15 winners at Toyota Park in Chicago, scoring six tries in the process. Ryan Jones's men led 27-3 at the break, and whilst Wales may have blown away the Americans in the Windy City on the scoreboard, they certainly didn't in the physicality stakes.

Davies proved a constant menace and raced over for a brace of tries to cap off an excellent tour. His power, in particular, and sleight of hand were clear for all to see, with his confidence growing with every minute. He said, 'It was a great tour and a real privilege to play for Wales. All of the boys have been great and the win over the USA made it a pleasing way to finish the season. Personally, I've had a great season and I'm now looking forward to the future.'

Duncan Jones, who finished the match as skipper after Ryan Jones suffered a head injury that ultimately prevented him from taking part in the Lions tour, said, 'All in all I'm pleased with the way things went. There are a few boys who took a few knocks so some people had to play out of position but they all stepped up to the mark.'

New Scarlets captain Mark Jones scored the first of his side's tries, Davies the second and after a penalty try had helped the tourists into a comfortable 27-3 lead, they consolidated after the break with Tom James crossing for a fourth, Cooper a fifth and Davies a sixth. It was a decent way to finish, although Wales also lost back-row forward Robin Sowden-Taylor to a hamstring tweak and wing Tom James to a shoulder injury. All that remains is to see if Welsh rugby can successfully help the rising players make the next significant step in their development.

Churchill Cup

by HUGH GODWIN

'The final scoreline of 49-22 secured a first Churchill Cup title to top off Irish rugby's stellar 2008-09 season but was chastening to England Saxons and their coaches'

There is no shortage of appetite for professional sport in Denver, Colorado. They have their Broncos, Rockies, Nuggets, Rapids, Mammoth and Avalanche in gridiron, baseball, basketball, Major League Soccer (MLS), lacrosse and ice hockey respectively – and rugby union can be added to this collection after the Mile High City hosted the seventh Churchill Cup in June 2009.

The withdrawal of Scotland A to take part in (and win) the Nations Cup in Romania allowed first-time entrants Georgia to join the USA, Canada, England Saxons, Ireland A and Argentina Jaguars in two pools of three teams, who played out three days of double-header matches at Infinity Park, Glendale. This is the USA's first municipally owned rugby ground and lies about 15 minutes' drive from downtown Denver, the self-styled 'Gateway to the Rockies'.

Ireland A finished top of Pool A and faced Pool B winners England Saxons on a concluding day of three finals – Cup, Plate and Bowl – at Dick's Sporting Goods Park, the 18,000-capacity stadium of the Colorado Rapids MLS side in Commerce City, situated in Denver's northwest outskirts. The seriousness of the Irish challenge was indicated by their A squad coming under the charge of the senior side's coaching panel of Declan Kidney, Gert Smal, Alan Gaffney and Les Kiss. Whereas England named one squad for their senior team's post-season Test series with Argentina and another for the Churchill Cup, the Irish retained ten players from their senior tour of North America for the second-string event staged solely in the USA for the first time.

England Saxons, the holders and four-times winners of the competition, fielded five full internationals – David Flatman, Nick Kennedy, Luke Narraway, Tom Varndell and Nick Abendanon – in their starting XV for the final, with a couple of what the Americans might describe as marquee players in Danny Cipriani and Shane Geraghty on the bench. The score stood at 10-9 to Ireland A after 20 minutes, and the England scrum, in which loose-head prop Flatman played all but a minute of his side's three matches, appeared to hold the whip hand. Then a missed penalty by the Saxons fly half Stephen Myler was followed quickly by a counterattack try by Ireland A scrum half Isaac Boss. The lead-up featured a storming run by centre Fergus McFadden and a short charge by hooker Sean Cronin. With the conversion by Johnny Sexton, recent hero of Leinster's Heineken Cup final win, the Irish had a 17-9 lead, which became 20-12 by half-time.

Perhaps it was the heat – temperatures nudged 115 degrees Fahrenheit, though it was, as the saying goes, the same for both sides – but something caused England to fall away badly. Cronin crashed over for Ireland A's third try 22 seconds into the second half as England dithered and lost the flight of the restart and the 6ft 11in Irish lock Devin Toner tidied up. Ireland A had 13 men to the Saxons' 14 at the time, in a match of two yellow cards to each side. Occasional thrusts by Abendanon and tries by flanker Ben Woods and wing Varndell were isolated English blows to a confident Ireland A captained by Northampton flanker Neil Best. In addition to the first-half scores by Toner and Boss and Cronin's

RIGHT Former Leicester clubmates Tom Varndell of England Saxons and Johne Murphy of Ireland A vie for a high ball in the final of the Cup in Commerce City, Denver, Colorado.

FACING PAGE USA prop Shawn Pittman shows intent as the Eagles beat Georgia 31-13 to win the Bowl final.

smart second-half opener, the Irish recorded tries through full back Felix Jones, wing Johne Murphy and replacement back-rower and squad skipper John Muldoon. The quality of distribution and pace of McFadden and Jones – the latter having just agreed to a move from Leinster to Munster – were boons to the Irish. Two of their six tries exposed England on the short side of the scrum.

'It was a massive challenge as, physically, England looked a lot bigger and stronger than us,' said Best. 'It was testament to our mentality that we brought it to them in the way we did.' The final scoreline of 49-22 secured a first Churchill Cup title to top off Irish rugby's stellar 2008-09 season but was chastening to England Saxons and their coaches Stuart Lancaster and Paul Hull. The Saxons players' extensive experience of the Guinness Premiership had not readied them automatically for the international arena. Myler of Northampton was man of the match in the decisive pool game against the USA, but he was mostly shackled by the Irish in the final and was replaced by Cipriani for the last 20 minutes, at which point the Saxons trailed 39-17. 'Both are quality players,' Lancaster said of his two No. 10s. 'I see both going on to be future internationals at fly half consistently for England and I imagine they'll battle it out for the next few years.'

Barbara O'Brien, the deputy governor of Colorado, joined incoming RFU president John Owen to present the Churchill Cup to the Irish. Denver is set to be the host city again in 2010, when the tournament could be a curtain-raiser for a Bledisloe Cup meeting between Australia and New Zealand. The humorous spectacle of hefty Georgian forwards lifting a female sports anchor in a line out on local TV helped drum up interest, and there were 9000 spectators for the pool matches at Infinity Park, while the finals at Dick's Sporting Goods Park drew a crowd of just over 5000. They saw Argentina Jaguars defeat Canada 44-29 to win the Plate, with centre Benjamín Urdapilleta kicking five conversions and three penalties. Urdapilleta's swishing left boot was almost on a par with anything Diego Maradona might have managed, but the Jaguars moved the ball through the hands just as sweetly. The wings Francisco Merello and Tomás De Vedia ran adventurously, and there were tries for hooker Agustín Creevy, Merello, Urdapilleta, De Vedia and back-row forward Leonardo Senatore. Canada's Matt Evans, a 21-year-old wing attending Hartpury College in England, scored two tries to top the tournament charts with four, and centre D.T.H. van der Merwe also crossed twice as a reward for his straight running and canny support play.

The Bowl was won by the USA against Georgia, 31-13, in a match accorded Test status. The Georgians were not at full strength, though, and in pool play at Glendale – the matches variously attracted hot sunshine, torrential rain, thunder and lightning – their hearty scrummaging offered rare solace during comprehensive defeats by Canada (42-10) and Ireland A (40-5). Ireland A scrum half

RIGHT The victorious Ireland A with the Churchill Cup after crushing England Saxons 49-22 in the final.

Boss, a 29-year-old veteran of 12 Ireland Tests, commented after the latter match: 'There are a lot of young boys here and it's our job to bring them through to the next stage.' The developmental nature of the competition was the primary concern for all the teams.

Ireland A's opening Pool A fixture – a 30-19 win over Canada – was a rematch of the teams' previous meeting in the 2007 Churchill Cup at Exeter in England. Now, with the Rocky Mountains providing the backdrop, Denis Hurley and McFadden scored first-half tries for the Irish. Even so they trailed 16-13 at half-time to two penalties and a drop by Ander Monro and the fly half's conversion of scrum half Phil Mack's dummy-and-go try. An Irish penalty try at a scrum and replacement front-rower Denis Fogarty's bonus-point score two minutes from the end turned it around.

In Pool B, England Saxons began with a hit-and-miss 28-20 win over Argentina Jaguars. With Cipriani's actress girlfriend, Kelly Brook, looking on and Infinity Park's 'Grubber Grille' and 'Shopping Maul' giving pun-loving spectators a chuckle, there were tries for wing Matt Smith, scrum half Joe Simpson and Varndell after the Jaguars had led 6-3 at half-time. The Saxons were on better form in a 56-17 romp against the USA. Kennedy, back in second-row action after missing London Irish's Guinness Premiership final through injury, scored from a terrible Eagles mix-up behind their goal line, and there were further tries for scrum half Micky Young, hooker Rob Webber, back-row Tom Guest, Varndell, Durban-born centre Brad Barritt and wing Noah Cato.

These players and others may have eyed the concurrent Lions tour or the preceding Six Nations Championship and wondered if they would follow the example of past Churchill Cup participants Rob Kearney, Keith Earls, Jamie Heaslip, Ugo Monye, Tom Croft, Lee Mears and Delon Armitage.

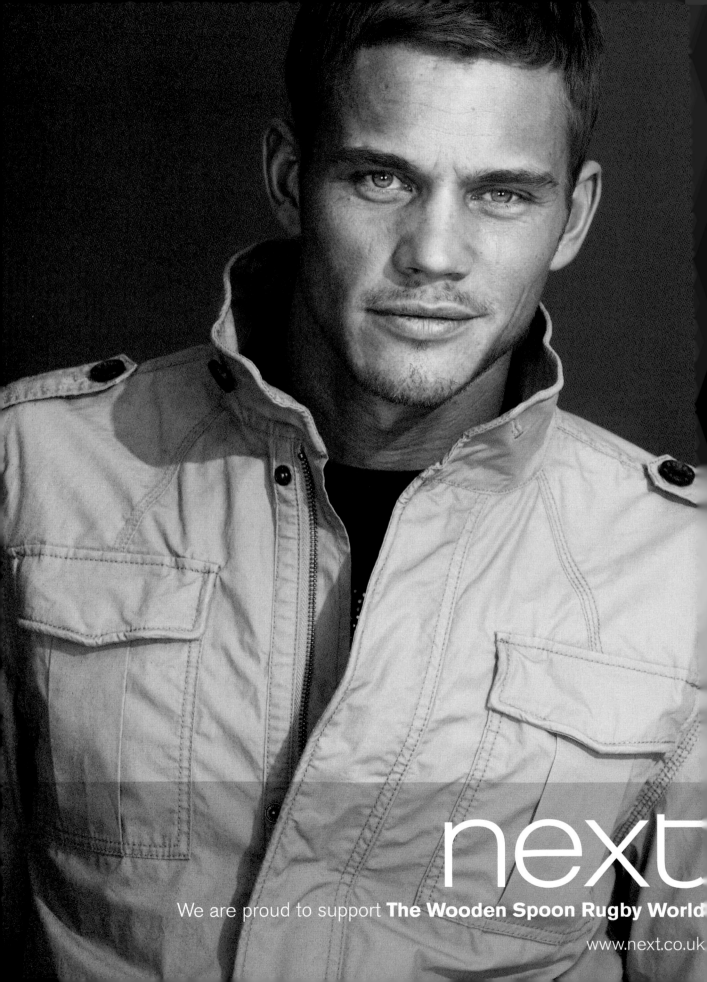

next

We are proud to support **The Wooden Spoon Rugby World**

www.next.co.uk

HOME FRONT

Expressing Themselves
Leicester Under Richard Cockerill

by **STEVE BALE**

'But the major surprise was Cockerill's decision on how Leicester would play their rugby: with an abandon that would have been regarded as sheer recklessness'

When Leicester last held sway over English rugby, with those four Premiership and two European titles culminating in the 'double double' of 2001 and 2002, Richard Cockerill would not have been the obvious candidate to lead them all the way back to where they were. But this is how it has transpired, the variable years of the mid- to late part of the decade seeing a succession of coaches tried. Many of these have been from outside the clannish family of Tigers, and most failed before the club went back to one of their own. Had this not been 'Cockers', it might have been obvious all along.

The signs are there that not only is the old hegemony being reimposed but this is being achieved with a style of rugby quite out of keeping with the memory of Cockerill as a pit-bull hooker for whom the niceties of rugby involved ruffling feathers on and off the field. Why, he has become part of the establishment, winner of the coach of the year award, even though he was only Heyneke Meyer's deputy until just after Christmas and caretaker for three months until the appointment was confirmed in April. 'It's slightly fraudulent I suppose, only having done it for a third of a year,' he said. 'I'll get the credit because I also get the blame, but it's not about me. It's about the club being successful. I'd much rather win a trophy for the team than me.'

So Leicester had their travails even last season, when they emerged triumphant domestically and fell at the final hurdle in the Heineken Cup as much through the exhaustion induced by the intensity of the weekly climax In April and May as their own small inadequacies. But it was also a harbinger of things to come, because for the first time in several years Leicester were able to go into a season, 2009-10, with a settled coaching team established from the previous season. As Cockerill himself said, 'It will help when for once you won't have a whole new coaching team coming in with a whole new set of ideas that players have to get used to. Stability will make a useful change.'

Not that Leicester exactly struggled between their defeat of Munster in the 2002 European final and their reappearance on the same stage last May, when they were defeated by Leinster – though their Heineken experiences do tell a story. Twice during the fallow years they qualified for the competition only through the back-door route of the Premiership wild card, a dubious, concocted arrangement which has

ABOVE Backs coach Matt O'Connor (centre) at a training session with kicking coach Paul Burke (left) and Heyneke Meyer, who stepped down as head coach in early 2009 because of family illness.

FACING PAGE Head coach Cockerill enjoys the moment as Leicester take the 2009 Guinness Premiership, having beaten London Irish in the final.

long since been abandoned. Mind, it would have been much worse if Leicester had failed to qualify altogether. There was the regular consolation of Premiership grand finals, though last May's defeat of London Irish was only the second victory in five of those Twickenham appearances.

It is fair to say that in Leicester of all places merely being in a final, as opposed to winning it, is virtually meaningless – a feeling Cockerill repeatedly put to his players when they were heading towards last season's finals. He should know: he sat on the bench behind another England hooker, Dorian West, in both of Leicester's winning Heineken Cup finals without ever taking the field.

So how did Leicester do it? How did they go from unlikely underachievers back to the best in England with years of promise lying ahead for a side in which the transition from old to new is again being done with minimum fuss and pain? First, by trial and error. When Cockerill was appointed, he was the sixth head coach or director of rugby Leicester had had in as many seasons, going back to Dean Richards, who was shown the door in 2004.

It should be remembered that the Richards halcyon years were themselves ushered in by a sacking – that of former Wallaby coach Bob Dwyer in 1998 – but the post-Richards era conclusively proved the drastic course is not always the best. John Wells, Pat Howard, Marcelo Loffreda and Meyer followed, and in the case of the latter three coaches departed at a rate of one a season. Another global search followed before Cockerill was given the job.

He came with a rough reputation. To begin with, there were legitimate questions about whether he was suited to the off-field role, the transfer-market wheeling and dealing that comes as a possibly disagreeable by-product of being in total charge. Cockerill was having none of it, not after being forwards coach under three head coaches and caretaker twice. 'You have to remember I have been the one who has been making decisions for quite a while now about which forwards we want and where we need to strengthen our pack,' he said. 'It's not exactly new.'

And so it began. But the major surprise was Cockerill's decision on how Leicester would play their rugby: with an abandon that would have been regarded as sheer recklessness when he was playing under Richards and captained by Martin Johnson. Leicester are still perfectly content to drive opponents into the dirt when they see fit, but the old ways are no longer the preferred ways. The Tigers have opened their minds and with it their rugby, though perhaps they are slightly wary of admitting as much. Here is England lock Ben Kay: 'People say it's all about an expansive game but it's not. It's about taking the game to the opposition and really challenging them. You can do that through the middle of the pitch as well.

'We've had moments in the past when we have played similar rugby, but where perhaps we stalled over the past couple of years was in being scared to go out and play. No longer.

'It's hardly been an innovation, just a change of attitude, and anyway perhaps people have tended to pigeon-hole us. It's still true, and always is, that some games have to be ground out.'

As Kay points out, Leicester have – maybe reluctantly given their traditional strength – gone some way in this direction before, specifically when Howard was their coach. He sought with some success to import to the East Midlands what he experienced at home in Australia.

Cockerill gallantly accords much of the credit for Leicester's expanded rugby to his backs coach Matt O'Connor, a Meyer appointee, and it is scarcely a coincidence that both O'Connor and Howard learnt much of their trade with the Brumbies in Canberra. 'I wouldn't know for sure because I didn't see a lot of Leicester in the Pat Howard era but I dare say it's a similar philosophy,' said O'Connor. 'The challenging thing, though, is always to turn the theory – which is easy enough to see – into practice.'

O'Connor actually plays down what has occurred as being more a changed attitude of mind than any great plan. 'The only real change is that we have simply encouraged the players to play and express themselves through their rugby,' he said.

RIGHT 'If you have Geordan Murphy, Aaron Mauger, Alex Tuilagi, you want to be using what they can give you.' Here Alesana Tuilagi evades Joe Carlisle to give the Tigers a try during their 2008-09 Premiership clash with Worcester Warriors at Welford Road. Leicester won the match 38-5.

'We have a very, very talented squad, a very gifted back line, and we wanted to give those guys opportunities to demonstrate their full skill set. For me it's always about the players you have. If you have Geordan Murphy, Aaron Mauger, Alex Tuilagi, you want to be using what they can give you.

'But encouraging that doesn't mean you don't encourage the other strengths of the team in relation to a very good set piece and hard work at the breakdown. We have some very gifted forwards as well.'

This, by extension, is a mild reproof to Meyer, and even to Loffreda before that. The Argentinian never really had a chance, arriving at Welford Road after the Pumas' third place at the 2007 World Cup and being sacked six months later after losing both the Premiership and Anglo-Welsh finals. Here was a fine example of getting there meaning next to nothing at Leicester. But the coup of recruiting Meyer after the South African Rugby Union had appointed Peter de Villiers ahead of him as Springbok coach did not seem so smart as Leicester muddled their way through the first half of last season.

'He was probably more conservative, more orientated to field position and not taking the same risks on the footy field,' said O'Connor. 'Cockers' experience at this club in a coaching capacity showed that most times Leicester lost was because they didn't play.

'With the players we had and the skills they had, we didn't want to be in that situation. It's a matter of putting maximum pressure on the opposition and sometimes that can be done by running, other times by kicking and a good set piece. We are lucky that there is a highly diverse skill set in that squad and that gives us variety and flexibility.'

When Meyer departed at the turn of the year, it was for reasons of serious family illness back home in Pretoria, and for a while he and Cockerill were in constant communication. But in the end Meyer resigned to be succeeded by Cockerill, and Leicester have plainly been the beneficiaries. Premiership rugby, never mind Europe, has never been so competitive, but Cockerill's Tigers have already resumed their place in the natural order of things.

Tigers Top the Tree
the 2008-09 Guinness Premiership
by CHRIS HEWETT

'Once again, the Premiership beggared belief in many respects. It was staggeringly punishing, yet there was more variety than critics of English club rugby would have you believe'

Thoroughly deserved in the sense that their late-season form under Richard Cockerill was both ruthless and professional in a typically Tigerish way, and just about deserved in respect of their narrow Twickenham grand final victory over London Irish, Leicester's success in the Guinness Premiership was hardly a bolt from the blue. They almost always find a way of being in the mix at the business end of a campaign, even when they reach the halfway point so far off the pace they can barely be seen without a good pair of binoculars.

Yet there were a couple of unexpected developments in what turned into the closest Premiership finish to date. One of them, the unpredictability of events at the top end of the table, was very welcome indeed. Both London Irish and Harlequins qualified for the play-offs, while hardy annuals like Gloucester and Wasps came up short. Football does not remotely threaten rugby in this regard, as the continuing hegemony of Manchester United, Liverpool, Chelsea and Arsenal demonstrates.

The other trend was far too football-like for comfort: namely, the rapid turnover of coaches and directors of rugby in the top flight of English union. Brian Smith left London Irish before the start of

ABOVE London Irish centre Delon Armitage cannot stop Jordan Crane of the Tigers from scoring the only try of the Guinness Premiership final, which ended 10-9 to Leicester.

FACING PAGE Tigers wing Scott Hamilton escapes the clutches of Exiles Mike Catt and Paul Hodgson at Twickenham.

the campaign (not that the Exiles were remotely happy about the way the Rugby Football Union went about luring their man into Martin Johnson's Red Rose set-up), while Heyneke Meyer, newly appointed as Leicester's top dog after the abrupt – some would say callous – removal of the respected Argentine tactician Marcelo Loffreda after half a season, disappeared back to South Africa a few days after Christmas. Family reasons were cited and Meyer certainly had illness issues to address, but there were also strong rumours of dissatisfaction with the team's progress under his stewardship.

Then the fun and games really started. Richard Hill, who had worked miracles on a minuscule budget, was elbowed out of Bristol; Eddie Jones walked out of Saracens in a rare old huff after the removal of chief executive Mark Sinderberry and the emergence of a new management regime of strong South African flavour; Ian McGeechan – yes, the great Lion himself – was hustled out of the door by Wasps; and Dean Ryan, who had taken Gloucester to consecutive top-of-the-table finishes in 2007 and 2008, lost his job at Kingsholm. With Philippe Saint-André leaving Sale for the rich man's pickings at super-wealthy Toulon, more than half the elite clubs saw changes at the top in the space of nine months.

This was carnage on a football scale. In fact, rugby has become worse than football in recent years. The job expectancy in the top position has shrunk to around 20 months – less than in soccer.

The statistics tell us more. Since the start of the 2004-05 season, approximately 40 individuals have performed director of rugby or head coach roles in a 12-team Premiership, with the best part of 30 changes of regime. Football, which operates on a 20-team format in the Premier League, has seen fewer than 60 different managers. The long-standing argument advanced by union stakeholders in England that football is the 'wrong model' for rugby's advancement seems just a little hollow all of a sudden.

Strange to relate, the big impacts at head coach level were made by two of the new boys: Toby Booth of London Irish, who took over the number one position when the RFU lured the highly regarded Smith away from the Madejski Stadium with promises of unfettered influence over international affairs, and Richard Cockerill, who was working under Meyer until the latter left for the Highveld. Cockerill made such a terrific job of the caretaker role that the Leicester board opted to abandon their worldwide search for a new leader and stay close to home instead.

Most people expected Booth to make a decent fist of it, for he had long been well thought of in coaching circles. (Indeed, Brian Ashton had earmarked him as an important member of a new England coaching team he would have put together had a few RFU grandees not brought about a change of regime after the 2008 Six Nations.) The Exiles did not begin particularly well, but they kick-started their season by winning a minor classic at Harlequins – their nearest and not-so-dearest

– in the fourth round of matches, coming from 20-3 down early in the second quarter to sneak home 28-27. It was the start of a six-match winning streak that featured utterly convincing victories over Sale and Gloucester, two of the teams confidently predicted to make the end-of-season play-offs.

There was much to admire about Irish as they established a bridgehead at the top end of the table: the contrasting brilliance of the Armitage brothers, Delon and Steffon, who would see their club form acknowledged by the England selectors; the Pacific Island power of Seilala Mapusua in midfield; the industrious work of Paul Hodgson at scrum half; the occasional flash of magical nostalgia from Mike Catt, still doing his thing after all these years. There were new faces, too: prop Alex Corbisiero looked a real find, as did strongly built wing Adam Thompstone.

Leicester, meanwhile, were having an odd time of it. After a decent start – their victory at Kingsholm on the opening day led to all sorts of ramifications at Gloucester, who had rather expected to win the game – they went through a seriously rough patch, winning only four times in ten Premiership starts between late September and mid-February. Yet once Cockerill found his bearings and reintroduced some time-honoured Tigers values to the mix (not to mention some thoroughly dependable Tigers personnel, like the outstanding Sam Vesty), things quickly came right. Their form at the back end of the campaign was exemplary and it propelled them all the way to the top of the log.

Elsewhere, there was strange work afoot in the forest. For instance, no one could quite get a handle on events at Gloucester. The team were doing comfortably enough to stay in contention for a top-four finish despite operating without a specialist open-side flanker for much of the campaign (long-term injuries to Andy Hazell and the explosive Fijian forward Akapusi Qera would have affected most sides, but the West Countrymen found a way to cope), yet there were constant rumblings of discontent deep below the surface. Questions over Ryan's future started to be asked publicly, there were clear signs that their major close-season signing Olly Barkley was yearning for a return to Bath, and there were equally unmistakeable smoke signals of the 'I want out' variety emanating from the Ryan Lamb camp. Something would have to give, it seemed, and it duly gave, big time. Gloucester's form collapsed over the final few rounds, and they missed out on the semi-finals by a couple of places.

Wasps? Well, they were another odd lot. More than any club, they allowed their knickers to become spectacularly twisted over the vexed issue of the Experimental Law Variations; indeed, McGeechan described the ELVs as 'anti-rugby' and ordered his charges to 'stop playing' in their own half of the field. Again, there were rumours of instability behind the scenes. The decision to allow both McGeechan and Shaun Edwards, the two principal members of the brains trust, to spend much of the season doing other things was the source of considerable disharmony at board level, and by the time Wasps discovered some of their customary late-season momentum, the door to the play-offs had been locked and bolted.

Down at the bottom, Bristol struggled from the off. The ELVs hurt Richard Hill's side more than any of the other Premiership clubs, not least because the West Countrymen had invested so much of themselves in developing a well-organised mauling game. With the maul effectively neutered by the new regulations, their heavyweight forwards were reduced to the equivalent of sporting eunuchs. Newcastle were also struggling, but with Tom May repositioned at outside half and deeply committed forwards like Phil Dowson and Geoff Parling working

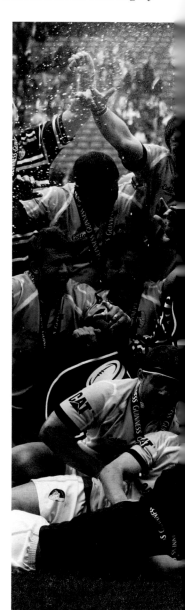

RIGHT The strip may be a little different from usual but the situation is familiar – Leicester Tigers are Guinness Premiership champions once again.

overtime for the cause, they saved themselves with something to spare. Their comprehensive victory over Bristol at the Memorial Ground was worthy of survival on its own.

Once again, the Premiership beggared belief in many respects. It was staggeringly punishing, yet there was more variety than critics of English club rugby would have you believe: for every tourniquet-tight 80 minutes' worth of bludgeoning rugby, there was a free-scoring festival of end-to-end excitement; and for every hard-working Chris Robshaw, the Harlequins flanker who tackled his way to a thoroughly deserved Guinness Premiership Player of the Season award, there was a thinking man's back like Joe Maddock, the Bath wing whose mature mastery of time and space was a joy to behold.

If the final at Twickenham failed to ignite, it was not because of any great flaw in the Premiership's rugby model. Some games will always be won on guts, on know-how, on the back of a little good fortune. Leicester had all those things going for them on the big day, and as a result they prevailed 10-9. Whatever the showpiece lacked in razzamatazz, it made up for in honest endeavour. The day the English club game loses that will be the day it loses itself.

Tony Hanks
From Wasps to Waikato – and Back

by CHRIS JONES

'What gives Hanks a fair chance of success is the fact that he already knows the club, having been originally brought over from New Zealand by Gatland in 2002'

Tony Hanks has been in rugby long enough to recognise a hospital pass. Taking over from Ian McGeechan as the London Wasps director of rugby was going to be a daunting task for any coach, but add to the equation the botched way the club handled the whole affair – played out in the media – and it turns Hanks's task into an even tougher assignment.

McGeechan was left with no option but to stand down after a period in charge that brought Heineken Cup and Guinness Premiership triumphs to follow on from the equally trophy-cabinet-filling period under Warren Gatland, who arrived after the giant strides made at the start of the

professional era with Nigel Melville in control, aided by John Mitchell. The list of former directors of rugby at the club reads like a Who's Who of the game, and now Hanks has to live up to that legacy.

What gives Hanks a fair chance of success is the fact that he already knows the club, having been originally brought over from New Zealand by Gatland in 2002 as a technical analyst and assistant coach for the side. Hanks was a key part of the coaching set-up that secured Wasps three Premiership titles, a Heineken Cup and Parker Pen Shield in just three seasons.

Hanks left the club in 2005, returning to New Zealand, where he took on the role of assistant coach with the Waikato provincial team, securing the Air New Zealand Cup in 2006 and the Ranfurly Shield a year later. Throughout 2006 and 2007, he also worked for the Chiefs Super 14 side as technical analyst and skills coach, combining the same role with the Junior All Blacks. In 2008 he was promoted to head coach of Waikato, a role he left to take over the reins at Wasps.

Hanks was at the club last season when Wasps needed help to keep the ship stable with McGeechan committed to selecting the Lions squad and head coach Shaun Edwards continuing his role as defence coach with Wales under Gatland. Hanks was seconded to Wasps between November and April. The club achieved an unbeaten run at home between December and the close of the season but failed to get high enough up the league to qualify for the Heineken Cup.

Hanks knows all about the weight of expectation involved with the job and said, 'I follow two pretty special coaches in Warren Gatland and Ian McGeechan – two guys that I have a huge amount of respect for. I feel very honoured to follow in their footsteps and I am thankful that I have not only had the opportunity to work with them but to learn from them both as well.

FACING PAGE New Wasps director of rugby Tony Hanks knows the club well, having served under Warren Gatland from 2002 to 2005 and acted as locum for Ian McGeechan in 2008-09.

ABOVE Wasps with the Heineken Cup after defeating Toulouse in the 2004 final. This was just one of five major trophies won in the Gatland/Hanks years.

'I came to Wasps in November with every intention of going back and resuming my Waikato commitments but the Wasps role was an opportunity too good to turn down. When I left Wasps, I always said that it would be great to be able to come back in some sort of capacity and what better than as director of rugby. Wasps is a well-respected club beyond the realms of the northern hemisphere and I am and always have been excited by the challenges that the Premiership and the European competitions bring.

'One of the big reasons for accepting the post has been the direction and ambition of the club, starting with Steve Hayes and Mark Rigby. I think it is important that a director of rugby has the support from his board and chairman and I believe we've got that. The club boasts an excellent support staff and a talented group of motivated players who I am looking forward to working with. For me it is important to mention Shaun. He is someone I have worked alongside throughout my entire Wasps career – he is a world-class coach and a great friend who I have great respect for.

'I know that coming to Wasps, you do so with a lot of expectation and rightly so, but for me this marks the start of a new era and the next chapter for Wasps – one that greatly excites me.'

With McGeechan considered surplus to requirements, the coaching set-up had to be changed under Hanks, and with Leon Holden heading back to New Zealand there needed to be a new forwards coach. That man is Trevor Woodman, the former England World Cup-winning prop, who has been living in Australia after injury forced a premature end to his career.

Woodman won 22 England caps and played for Bath, Gloucester and Sale before injury compelled him to quit the sport at just 29. He worked with Sydney University and was then recruited by the Australian Rugby Union to work on scrums with the Wallabies and the Super 14 franchises. He said, 'Wasps have an unbeatable record in the game with an honours list that can rival any other Premiership club and over the years they have produced some of the game's most exciting talents.

'For me personally and professionally I am hugely excited by the challenge that lies ahead – the club is at the beginning of its next chapter and working alongside great coaches in Tony Hanks and Shaun Edwards you can sense the determination and the desire to make this season a success from the off – something I am delighted to have an opportunity to be a part of.

'Wasps have always been one of those clubs whether as a player, coach or spectator, you had an immense amount of respect for. Taking on the role of forwards coach, I will have the opportunity to not only work as part of this great establishment, but also join forces with some of the most respected names in the game with the likes of Vickery and Shaw – two of my former England team-mates.'

Also on board for next season is John McCloskey, who has huge experience in Gaelic sport and will be tasked with improving the kicking game at the club along with other key skills areas. Hanks is bullish about McCloskey's appointment and added, 'The addition of John to our set-up sees the introduction of a new role dedicated to the strengthening and development of our players' core skills. To have someone solely focused in this area we show a commitment to long-term development and in John we have a man with a proven coaching ability and great record in Gaelic sport.

'His strengths around handling, aerial skills and kicking are key aspects of the modern game and I think that the appointment will be of great benefit to our squad across the board. Having worked with John last season I was very impressed with what he had to offer and I believe that his appointment will add great value to the Wasps squad in the short- and long-term future.'

And with Wasps' proud record, Hanks knows that future has to bring trophies.

ABOVE Trevor Woodman (right) and Phil Vickery (left) pack down for Gloucester in 2004. The opposition are Wasps, for whom Woodman and Vickery will team up once again in 2009-10.

FACING PAGE As assistant coach at Waikato under Warren Gatland, Hanks helped the union to the inaugural Air New Zealand Cup in 2006 and to the Ranfurly Shield in 2007. Here Marty Holah heads for the line against North Harbour in the 2007 Ranfurly Shield challenge, which Waikato won 52-7.

Leinster Deliver the 2009 Heineken Cup Final

by MARK SOUSTER

'Yet led by O'Driscoll Ireland won the Grand Slam in heart-stopping fashion. Perhaps it was inevitable then that the vapour trail should stretch onwards and upwards to Edinburgh'

Virtually every year the Heineken Cup throws up drama, emotion and riveting competition, and in that regard the 2009 tournament will stand comparison with the best. In many ways Europe's premier club competition is not unlike the Grand National in that invariably a heartwarming story accompanies the winner. This season was no different. Leinster's first success provided a notable and belated domestic and international double for Brian O'Driscoll in the autumn of his superlative career, and a one-season wonder, for all the right reasons, in Rocky Elsom. And do not forget Leicester's wonderful dignity in defeat, which epitomised the very essence of good sporting conduct.

In future years when rugby historians thumb the record books, 2009 will resonate with the names of O'Driscoll and Elsom. That is not to belittle, denigrate or downplay the efforts of the whole Leinster side, ably led by Leo Cullen and coached by Michael Cheika, but no one can deny that in tandem those two provided the stardust, the magic.

Leicester's situation as the only club to have defended successfully their European title gives them a unique pedigree. In contrast Leinster have been stereotypical underachievers, a side which when it really mattered failed conspicuously to deliver. Few of their supporters need reminding of the succession of near misses, most markedly the loss to Munster in the 2006 knockout stages. More of the same was predicted this year, not least on the basis of Munster's ruthless last-eight destruction of the Ospreys at Thomond Park. But Leinster's semi-final success at Croke Park proved to be their Damascene moment, when massive self-doubt was replaced by massive self-belief.

ABOVE Leicester Tiger Tom Croft tries to slow down Heineken Cup final man of the match Rocky Elsom of Leinster.

FACING PAGE No-side at Murrayfield and Brian O'Driscoll and Rob Kearney can barely believe it – a Six Nations Grand Slam and Heineken double for Ireland and Leinster.

Much could be said about Ireland over the past few years. Yet led by O'Driscoll Ireland won the Grand Slam in heart-stopping fashion in Cardiff. Perhaps it was inevitable then that the vapour trail should stretch onwards and upwards to Edinburgh, the venue for the Heineken Cup final. Given O'Driscoll's lustre, the betting would have been on the centre wrapping up his annus mirabilis with a Lions victory in South Africa. It was not to be, but two out of three is not a bad return.

Leinster's resolve may well have sprung from the resentment at being described as 'ladyboys' by Neil Francis, the former Ireland lock. Francis, a Leinsterman himself, made his comment at Christmas after defeat at Castres threatened to derail yet another campaign. It can be seen as a turning point. After beating Leicester 19-16 at Murrayfield, O'Driscoll was quick to refer to what he described as distasteful remarks. 'We haven't forgotten those things,' he said. 'This was the one I wanted above all the others. It's been ten years coming and it's with your pals. This is a very tightknit group with no hierachy. That togetherness and resilience got us through.'

For years O'Driscoll has been a superstar of the game, a player admired and feared in equal measure. He has overcome serious injury and is still plagued by hamstring and shoulder trouble, but you would never really guess it on the field, where he is a Catherine wheel of energy, off whom sparks fly. He leads and others have to follow.

Less was known of Elsom. Cheika, whose own career at Leinster might have been in doubt had the province again come up short, had signed the no-nonsense Australian on a year's contract. He was touted as the missing link. But could one man really have such a galvanising influence on a side? Quite simply, yes. For whatever reason Elsom felt he needed time out from his homeland, a sabbatical in Dublin seemed to provide the answer. It certainly provided the stimulation, but then the Irish capital has that effect on most people.

Elsom admitted that he had not known quite what to expect, but his sojourn had exceeded all expectations. 'It could not have been more different,' said Elsom. 'Things were looking grim mid-season. But we got ourselves back on track and in the last three games there was a lot of clarity about what we wanted to do. This was bigger than anything back home.'

Despite a charm offensive, Elsom could not be persuaded to stay on. His heart lay in Australia and having given his word to the ARU he has returned home to rejoin the Wallabies. But he departed in the best possible

LEFT Leicester flanker Ben Woods drives for the line to score his side's try just before half-time. Scrum half Julien Dupuy converted to add to his two first-half penalties and give the Tigers a 13-9 lead at the interval.

manner, having provided wonderful memories and with the crowd baying for more. It was fitting that he was both Leinster's player of the year and also the man of the match at Murrayfield. O'Driscoll was unstinting in his praise of the flanker and his performance just days after he had walked away unscathed from a car accident. 'We wouldn't have won the Heineken Cup without Rocky Elsom,' O'Driscoll said. 'He is a remarkable player, probably the best player I have ever played with and I have played with some very good players. He doesn't make that many errors, has a massive work rate and his ball-carrying is frightening.'

All of Elsom's attributes were necessarily in evidence in the final as Leinster staged a remarkable comeback to deny Leicester a hat-trick of Heineken Cup triumphs. The match was not a spectacle but lost nothing in its absorbing intensity and in the ebb and flow of the respective fortunes of two sides desperate not to lose. After their end-of-season exertions and their Premiership final success, this was a game too far for the English champions. They gave everything but simply ran out of steam and ideas if not kamikaze-like commitment.

Leinster had looked liked like paying for their failure to make the most of their opening-quarter dominance, a period in which Leicester's line out was reduced to a shambles, not least by Elsom, and only committed defence kept the Irish out. By half-time, though, it was Leinster who were hanging on after Stan Wright's sin-binning and having gone behind to a Ben Woods try. Julien Dupuy converted and added a 43rd-minute penalty to make it 16-9 to Leicester. Not many sides come back from a seven-point deficit against the Tigers, and Elsom admitted that Leinster's defence had lost its shape temporarily, which allowed Dan

Hipkiss to reinforce his credentials as a line-breaking centre of quality, one who on occasion managed to embarrass O'Driscoll. Nevertheless, having reorganised their defensive lines, Leinster recovered their poise and sense of purpose.

Although the talismanic figure of Felipe Contepomi was unavailable for the final, having been injured against Munster in the semis (he has now joined Philippe Saint-André's Toulon revolution), Johnny Sexton proved a capable, accurate and match-winning understudy. The young out-half has always been highly regarded and made his mark with a dropped goal from 50 metres – to add to O'Driscoll's own opening salvo – and kicked a penalty, before Jamie Heaslip's converted try levelled the scores around the 50-minute mark. Even then, Leicester remained ferocious at the breakdown, counter-rucking with an almost insane desperation, and continued to force Leinster to work hard for every scrap of possession. Extra time looked possible until Sexton slotted the winning kick with nine minutes left on the clock. Leicester lost nothing in defeat. Their sporting acceptance expressed through Richard Cockerill, their head coach, and their own salute as the trophy was presented was commendable in the despair of defeat.

'We're disappointed that we lost, obviously, but it was a tight game. We couldn't have given any more, could we? The boys played their hearts out. No complaints. You accept winning, you have to accept losing. Of course we want to win. I am not a great loser but you have to be dignified in defeat and that's us.' In hindsight such grace could have done more for Leicester's image than another victory. After the less-than-glorious involvment with Marcelo Loffreda and Heyneke Meyer, the Tigers have successfully turned to one of their own – but an individual who belies his reputation and who sees the bigger picture. He is the frontman the club have been searching for. With Cockerill at the helm they will go far.

**883,839 players. 57,000 teams.
9,810 clubs. 4 nations.
Behind one shirt.**

www.lionsrugby.com/hsbc

EVEN GREATER TOGETHER

PRINCIPAL PARTNER

Saints Seal Return
the 2009 Challenge Cup Final

by TERRY COOPER

'One season without European competition could easily have dulled Northampton's competitive edge, but they went through their group from early October like a fireball'

Northampton's achievement in winning the European Challenge Cup with a comfortable 15-3 success against Bourgoin at the Twickenham Stoop was, in many ways, as admirable as the more high-profile triumphs of Leinster and Leicester in the Heineken and Premiership competitions. For the Saints to claim a prize in their first season after promotion was remarkable. One season without European competition could easily have dulled Northampton's competitive edge, but they went through their group from early October like a fireball, with half-century hammerings of Toulon, Montpellier and Bristol. Saints made it eight wins for English teams in the last nine years of this second-tier event.

Not for the first time a French club let themselves down in the final, which soon reached the level of an old-fashioned, violent Anglo-French running fight. There were several private combats before Northampton flanker Neil Best and Bourgoin scrum half Morgan Parra were sin-binned for initiating a more general brawl in the 35th minute. Then, five minutes from time with the result decided, Courtney Lawes, replacement lock, perpetrated a borderline, unpenalised late tackle on Parra. Unfortunately, it resulted in a dislocated shoulder, and French rage erupted in instant, ferocious retribution from Thomas Genevois. Having not long ago arrived as a substitute, Genevois punched Lawes twice in the face, rightly receiving a red card. Meanwhile, French captain Julien Frier whacked Euan Murray, who had already had his eye bloodied by an earlier assault. Murray nobly resisted the urge to retaliate to protect his Lions tour place.

ABOVE Referee Clancy shows Neil Best the yellow card in the 35th minute.

FACING PAGE Stephen Myler slots the second of his five out of five penalty kicks.

PAGE 107 Bourgoin skipper Julien Frier prevents a try by Saints wing Paul Diggin.

Frier's punch went unseen by referee George Clancy, but the Bourgoin skipper was cited for it and appeared alongside his colleague at a disciplinary hearing in Dublin. There both Frier and Genevois were given three-week suspensions. Their offences were rated only in the 'middle range' of seriousness for striking an opponent. Especially in the case of Genevois, who went back for seconds while Lawes was being held, the penalties seemed lenient. You would not want a friend of yours to be the victim of punches in the higher range of seriousness.

To compound the players' disgrace, Bourgoin assistant coach Xavier Péméja stated, in fine football manager's mode, 'I did not see the punch,' which occurred ten yards from his touch line. He added, 'The late tackle that started the trouble should always be a sending-off. A punch is only a sin-bin.' Oh, is it? That's news to the International Board. But he was right when he said 'The referee's first duty is to protect the players.' In general, though, Bourgoin were ill-disciplined, conceding 15

penalties to seven, enabling Stephen Myler to win the match. As well as repeatedly, illegally spoiling Northampton's close-range, potentially try-scoring opportunities, Bourgoin were depressingly limited. They hinted at a try a mere twice, in keeping with their abysmal try record this season.

Northampton's director of rugby, former Sale Sharks and England Saxons coach Jim Mallinder, said, 'There are some battered players, but the bruises don't hurt so much when you win. We gave

this cup run everything and now we are back in the top tier, where we deserve to be. We kept our discipline and I am especially pleased with Dylan Hartley, who is frequently targeted, but he showed again that he can restrain himself and keep his head.'

Saints favourite Tom Smith, the Scotland and Lions veteran, was given the final few minutes as a farewell to rugby. He said, 'There are mixed emotions, but to end with the club winning silverware was truly special. There will be higher expectations next season. That was step one, and hopefully steps two, three and four will come in the next few years.'

Captain Bruce Reihana commented, 'I will smile all summer. We fought for everything. There have been highs and lows at the club, but this is a true high.' Meanwhile, Hartley noted, 'You want to compete with the major teams on the best grounds. That's our reward.'

One weakness in the European tournaments is that the French regard their domestic leagues as more important. English sides that fail to make the Heineken Cup target the Challenge Cup as a route to performing at that higher level, especially when they are struggling in the Premiership and the Challenge Cup is the only way of qualifying. That was the case for four of the five English quarter-finalists this time – Saints, Newcastle, Saracens and Worcester. By finishing eighth in the Premiership, Northampton had to win the Challenge Cup final to play in the 2009-10 Heineken Cup. Wasps had finished seventh in the Premiership and, with justifiable self-interest, wanted Bourgoin to win the cup in order to take the seventh Heineken place allocated to England.

Myler kicked five goals from five shots, making him the runaway leading scorer in the tournament with 133 points. His penalties came in the eighth, 17th, 37th, 48th and 59th minutes. Parra's 33rd-minute goal was a pitiful return for the Frenchmen. But defences were supreme, as exemplified in Bourgoin's making 28 tackles in the move before Northampton's first score. Despite the absence of tries, there was tons of handling, and a merciful lack of aerial tennis. Northampton provided the overwhelming bulk of the ball-carrying, but Bourgoin always had tacklers available. If only their attacking vision had matched the resources of the defence. Myler's form brought him selection for the Churchill Cup, where he went on to compete with Danny Cipriani for the England Saxons No. 10 position.

Bourgoin had somehow scraped into the knockout stages, despite losing twice to Italian side Petrarca Padova and once to Worcester in the pool matches. In the knockout stages, they defeated London Irish and Worcester to reach the final. Northampton saw off Connacht and Saracens in the quarters and semis after whitewashing their group.

"Wishing the Wooden Spoon every success with their ongoing work"

The **Saracens Sport Foundation** aims to inspire communities and change lives through the power of sport. Through the Saracens brand, professional players and high quality staff, we engage and challenge children and young people to lead an active, healthy and rewarding lifestyle.

To find out more about the work of the Saracens Sport Foundation and how you can support our work, visit **www.saracens.com/foundation** or call us on **01707 268 919**

SARACENS SPORT FOUNDATION

REVIEW OF THE
SEASON 2008-09

Greenwash
the 2009 Six Nations Championship
by CHRIS JONES

'Thanks to tries from Brian O'Driscoll and wing Tommy Bowe, the Irish got back on track. Then a Ronan O'Gara dropped goal with a couple of minutes to go won the game for Ireland'

Having endured numerous false dawns and ruined 'big days', Ireland finally ended a 61-year wait for Grand Slam glory and landed their first RBS Six Nations title in typically nerve-jangling fashion in Cardiff. A last-gasp 50-metre kick by Stephen Jones that would have won the game for Wales seemed certain to creep over the crossbar at the Millennium Stadium and send the Irish players off to their regular psychiatrists, where the question 'Why does it always happen to us?' would again be discussed.

However, the ball dipped under the bar – not over it – and Ireland had won 17-15, leaving the former champions to reflect on why Jones – who had played the entire match and must have been exhausted – had been given the kick, rather than Gavin Henson or even James

Hook, who was sitting on the replacements' bench but not called into action. Ireland had trailed 6-0 at half-time to keep their thousands of fans in the stadium in a terrible state, but thanks to tries from Brian O'Driscoll, their inspirational captain, and wing Tommy Bowe, who would be a revelation on the summer Lions tour to South Africa, the Irish got back on track. Then a Ronan O'Gara dropped goal with a couple of minutes to go won the game for Ireland after Wales had led 15-14. O'Gara also kicked both conversions, while the Welsh relied on four Stephen Jones penalties plus his own dropped goal kicked just moments before O'Gara's. O'Gara is now the highest points scorer in the championship's history, taking over from Jonny Wilkinson.

Declan Kidney, the new Ireland head coach, rightly received plenty of praise in a season that also saw Leinster win the Heineken Cup and Paul O'Connell selected as Lions captain to South Africa. With their victory in Wales, Ireland finally had a team to stand alongside Karl Mullen's side of 1948 and consigned the defending Grand Slam champions to a fourth-place finish, with England, under

new team manager Martin Johnson, finding themselves in second place, having been afflicted by 'yellow fever' for much of the tournament. France were third, courtesy of their big victory over Italy in Rome, while Scotland just stayed ahead of winless Italy. It wasn't enough to keep Frank Hadden in the Scottish head coach role, and it now falls to former England head coach Andy Robinson to try and find a way of making Scotland truly competitive and regular winners despite their lack of playing numbers.

It had all started frantically for the Irish with a 30-21 home win over France at Croke Park, Dublin, an arena that Ireland have embraced with enthusiasm, and with 82,000 roaring their support, it was a strong opener. Jamie Heaslip, Brian O'Driscoll and Gordon D'Arcy ran in tries as the Irish registered their first triumph against France for six years. O'Gara chipped in with 15 points as the Irish dominated the final quarter. A scrappy display in Rome saw the Irish record a 38-9 success, and then came the single-point win over England, 14-13, in Dublin that was much closer than the play warranted thanks to a very late English try. This was the match many would look back on as evidence that Ireland were still capable of messing up under pressure, while it also proved England were not the basket case their poor disciplinary record suggested.

Ireland had turned up in Cardiff on the back of a 22-15 win over Scotland at Murrayfield that saw Jamie Heaslip power over for a try created by a moment of brilliance from Peter Stringer. Heaslip, the Leinster No. 8, burst into the match with a point to prove and the Lions selectors took note, duly handing him the Test jersey against the Springboks. But there was no place on tour for the veteran Stringer, who had turned this particular game around. The Irish needed this winning momentum and it was just enough to take them over the line against Wales in a final match made for television.

England, having started the process in November, continued to collect yellow cards – plus the resulting ten minutes in the sin bin – with real abandon. Goode got one in the 23-15 loss to Wales in Cardiff, as did Mike Tindall, in a match Johnson's men could have won. The yellow cards became a very unfunny joke, and when Danny Care needlessly shoved an Irish player in the back at Croke Park to collect England's tenth card in four games, the cameras caught Johnson's fury. Johnson's decision to entrust England's tactical play to Brive-based Andy Goode for the first two games highlighted the need to kick points and play a tactical kicking game, rather than put any faith in Danny Cipriani. The Wasps No. 10 was discarded after the poor autumn run and would not feature at all, as Toby Flood, when fit, became the alternative to Goode.

England bounced back superbly from the Welsh and Irish reverses to beat France 34-10 – with Flood to the fore – and Scotland, who had not won at Twickenham since 1983. England regained the Calcutta Cup, winning 26-12, thanks to tries from Ugo Monye, Riki Flutey and Mathew Tait. Toby Flood contributed eight points with the boot and Danny Care dropped a goal. Monye's score was his first in Tests and he had already stopped Thom Evans scoring with a brilliant cover tackle – these were two pieces of skill that would win him a place on the Lions tour.

That England finally got their act together was thanks, in no small part, to their decision to recall lock Simon Shaw. This enabled captain Steve Borthwick to concentrate on his line-out work without the worry of trying to be a ball carrier and strongman – roles he is not best suited to perform at the highest level. Significantly, Shaw went on the Lions tour to South Africa that summer, but neither Borthwick nor Nick Kennedy – originally chosen ahead of Shaw for England – was selected to join him. With their second-row balance back, England finished strongly, and playing on the front foot meant fewer penalties and no yellow cards. Hooray!

France, meanwhile, ended with that 50-8 defeat of Italy, which left the Azzurri with the Wooden Spoon and a fourth RBS Six Nations whitewash. A burst of three tries in six minutes in the first half helped give the French a 25-3 lead at the break, Sébastien Chabal, François Trinh-Duc and Maxime Médard touching down, with Cédric Heymans, Thomas Domingo, Médard again and Julien Malzieu completing the try-fest and Morgan Parra kicking 15 points. It was yet another example of how good the French could be – as they had been in beating Wales 21-16 in Paris – yet they fell badly at Twickenham. They would then win against the All Blacks in Dunedin in the summer without some key players to continue to cling onto their image as the most unpredictable side in world rugby.

Against Wales, controversial coach Marc Lièvremont had given a debut to 20-year-old Mathieu Bastareaud in midfield, with Benoît Baby, usually a centre, positioned at fly half and novice Morgan Parra handed the goal-kicking duties. All three responded well. Lièvremont continues to be the 'tinkerman' of world rugby, but there is no doubting the depth of talent in the French game. All they need is consistency in both performance and selection.

Wales were not the efficient outfit we had seen in the previous championship and needed Tom Shanklin's late try as a replacement to beat Italy 20-15 and keep their title hopes alive for that final match against the Irish. Against the Italians, Shane Williams scored his forty-sixth Test try, while James Hook kicked ten points in a side that controversially showed nine changes from the one beaten by France in Paris. Alun-Wyn Jones became the youngest forward to captain Wales since 1934, while the previous season's Grand Slam skipper, Ryan Jones, was named as a replacement. Head coach Warren Gatland had to send on the cavalry up front in prop Gethin Jenkins, hooker Matthew Rees and Jones. Wales trailed 15-13 with nine minutes left, but Shanklin saved the day.

Despite also beating the Scots (26-13) and the English, Wales had seen their title hopes badly hurt – and those of first back-to-back Grand Slams since 1909 snuffed out – in Paris on a Friday night. (Yes, we have started playing Six Nations matches on that evening.) Ryan Jones missed a key tackle on Imanol Harinordoquy, and the Welsh run of eight successive Six Nations victories came to an end, France winning the match 21-16. Lee Byrne again impressed that night, while two Wales players who later offered themselves as key components of the

BELOW Maxime Médard looks overjoyed as Cédric Heymans touches down in France's 21-16 win over Wales in Paris.

FACING PAGE Mark Cueto outstrips Morgan Parra to score England's first try in the opening minute against France.

PAGE 120 Paul Griffen (on ground) and Marco Bortolami struggle to slow down Jason White as Scotland defeat Italy 26-6 at Murrayfield.

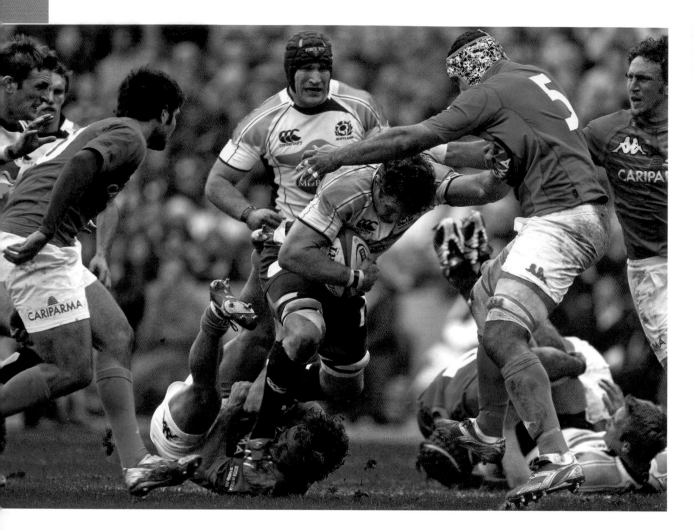

Lions Test side were prop Adam Jones, who made great strides in the championship, and scrum half Mike Phillips, who returned from a knee injury to prove he is the best No. 9 in Europe.

The one day when Scots fans could feel their side really were fully fledged members of the Six Nations, rather than making up the numbers, came against Italy, the team who are going backwards in terms of player quality and performance. It must hurt captain Sergio Parisse hard to be part of such a poor side when he is of world class. Simon Danielli scored one of the tries of the tournament and set up Scott Gray for another as the Scots grabbed a much-needed 26-6 boost at Murrayfield before losing against Ireland and at Twickenham to end Hadden's reign.

The Italians, meanwhile, could not give their coach, Nick Mallett, much to smile about. It was Mallett, however, who had helped give England a winning start by asking Mauro Bergamasco to switch from his normal flanker's role to solve an injury crisis at scrum half. The first half against England was hard to bear for any rugby fan as Bergamasco had a horror show and appeared to be, by some way, the worst scrum half to ever turn out in an international match at Twickenham. It was a huge gamble by the Italians and one that left them open to accusations of bringing the game into disrepute as they lost 36-11. The Italian campaign then ended in that heavy defeat by France, with little in between to suggest the Azzurri are any nearer parity with any other country but Scotland. After Murrayfield, even that is now in question. When Mirco Bergamasco scored Italy's try against England in the opening game, it was a false dawn for their back play. Italy, even under Mallett, are still a huge pack with one-dimensional ideas about how to beat opponents. Stand up to their physical battering and keep a close eye on Parisse and you have them under lock and key. Just as Ireland have that Grand Slam, Six Nations trophy and Triple Crown.

The Club Scene
England: Up and Down Again
by BILL MITCHELL

'In early December Oxford and Cambridge competed in what many people considered to be the best Varsity Match ever. The Blue teams shared eight tries'

Rugby nations are judged by their showcases – that is, their national teams – and for the latest campaign England's results were equivocal: a disastrous showing in November was followed by a very big improvement in the Six Nations. They took second place in the latter, with any fortune that was going favouring the opposition – notably Ireland (the champions and Grand Slammers) and Wales, both of whom dominated the final selection for the summer's Lions tour of South Africa.

ABOVE Oxford University players are ecstatic as referee Wayne Barnes brings the 2008 Varsity Match to a close. The Dark Blues hung on at the end to win a riveting contest 33-29.

EDF Energy Intermediate Cup Winners 2009

November's side played four matches at Twickenham and lost three of them, the Pacific Islands being the only visitors to lose (39-13). Australia managed to recover from a losing position to win 28-14, then South Africa, who had been lucky the previous week that a Paterson-less Scotland missed a series of easy kicks, turned on the style for a record 42-6 defeat of the men in white. The final autumn international against New Zealand was little more than a damage-limitation exercise as the hosts went down 32-6.

Nevertheless, come the Six Nations Martin Johnson's side performed better, with the enthusiasm of recent arrivals like the Armitage brothers and good performances from the likes of Tom Croft. The positives from the tournament were comfortable wins over Italy (36-11), Scotland (26-12) and France (34-10), while away defeats in Cardiff (23-15) and Dublin (14-13) owed much to bad luck, as averred to above, but also to a continued lack of discipline – too many yellow cards. Get this right and a Grand Slam in 2010 is a real possibility.

Defeat to the Barbarians (33-26), a victory at Old Trafford against Argentina (37-15) followed by defeat once again in Argentina (24-22) with teams depleted by the Lions tour were of little relevance. Overall five wins from 12 outings going back to November was a misleading story and 2009-10 may well confirm that to be a false impression, but

it will require some help from the major clubs for talented English players to come through. With their interests understandably being in favour of their own results and league positions, the clubs' signings have been from many national backgrounds, not necessarily English.

Among the clubs, the most notable winners were Leicester, who triumphed 10-9 against London Irish in the Guinness Premiership final but could not make it a double, losing 19-16 to Leinster the following weekend in the final of the Heineken Cup. Northampton beat Bourgoin 15-3 to take home the European Challenge Cup; Gloucester, though, came badly unstuck against Cardiff, 50-12, in the final of the EDF Energy Cup, the Anglo-Welsh competition. In the purely English knockout contests, meanwhile, Moseley won the EDF Energy National Trophy final 23-18 against Leeds Carnegie, Hartpury College won the EDF Energy Intermediate Cup final 41-31 against Clifton, while Cullompton and Brighton picked up the Senior and Junior Vases respectively.

Lancashire won the Bill Beaumont Cup for the County Championship, the Army won the Inter-Services competition and GKT the Hospitals Cup. Meanwhile, Rosslyn Park continued to play excellent

ABOVE Moseley full back Andy Binns, in his final season with the club, scores in the EDF Energy National Trophy final.

FACING PAGE, TOP Hartpury College celebrate winning the EDF Energy Intermediate Cup. The Gloucestershire outfit returned to Twickenham the next week to win the BUCS title.

FACING PAGE, BOTTOM Former England wing David Rees in action for Clifton against Hartpury College at Twickenham.

2p to Wooden Spoon.

Every time someone murders a bankers.

 Wooden Spoon

Wickwar Brewing Company. Proud sponsor of Wooden Spoon

counter-culture.org.uk

hosts to the Schools Sevens tournament, with Millfield winning both the Open competition and the Colts event.

Arguably Twickenham's best game of the season deserves a paragraph of its own. In early December Oxford and Cambridge competed in what many people considered to be the best Varsity Match ever. The Blue teams shared eight tries, Oxford emerging as narrow winners, 33-29, despite a gallant Cambridge fightback from a 28-10 deficit. As it was, the Dark Blues had the man of the match – of many games for that matter – in Tim Catling, who crossed the Cambridge line three times in the first half. For those wanting to enjoy the Twickenham experience, there could have been no better way than by seeing this Varsity Match!

> **ABOVE** Oxford wing Tim Catling completes his first-half hat-trick in the Varsity Match. It was the first individual three-try performance in the fixture since Ken Fyfe for Cambridge in 1934.

The most exciting moments of 2008-09 came after the season had ended – in July to be exact – when England were chosen to host the 2015 Rugby World Cup. Several venues other than Twickenham will be used – mostly soccer grounds – and the Millennium Stadium in Cardiff is also expected to be allowed to stage some matches. England were selected for 2015 in preference to Japan, who have been awarded the event in 2019, when it is hoped they may be able to field a team capable of reaching the last eight, the least one might expect from a host nation.

Footnote

If the Lions tour has left any legacy, it is that certain things in the game are totally unacceptable, with a Springbok being suspended for eye-gouging and a Lion being similarly punished after using his knees in a tackle. While the latter may have been an accident, the first offence certainly was not, even if the Springbok coach supported his player. In each case a red rather than a yellow card seemed to be appropriate, and in each case the referee earned few marks for taking the easy option. What's more, the Springboks seemed all too ready to resort to fisticuffs, and the laws of the game provide for – and perhaps should stipulate – a red card in such cases. Gratuitous violence does nothing for the reputation of the game.

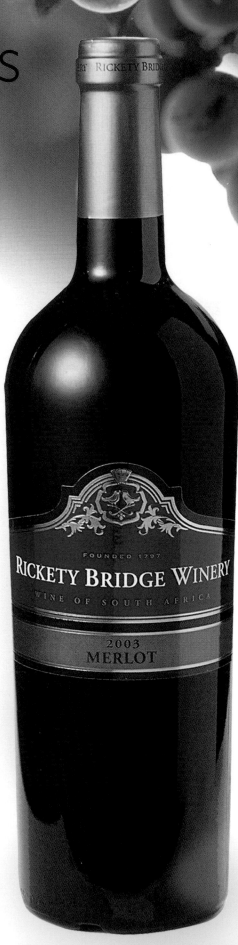

Scotland: Edinburgh in the Ascendant   by ALAN LORIMER

'Realisation of Edinburgh's real potential came later in the season, when the club made a late charge with six successive wins, which included two against Cardiff'

It was the season in which Edinburgh finally showed their true worth, and in a not unconnected way it was the season in which former England coach Andy Robinson completed his rehabilitation from the low point of 2006. Robinson, in his second season with Edinburgh, guided the capital side to the runners-up position in the Magners League, the best ever placing by a Scottish club in the Celtic competition, and in so doing made himself the frontrunner to take over from Frank Hadden as Scotland coach. It was no surprise, then, when Robinson was appointed to the Scotland job. Certainly no surprise at the Edinburgh club, where Robinson had earned the affection of his squad with a new approach that gave the capital men a (previously missing) harder edge and winning mentality.

The turnabout, however, did not occur early enough in the season to prevent Edinburgh from yet again disappointing in the Heineken Cup, in a campaign that included double defeats by both Leinster and Wasps but chalked up home and away successes against Castres. Once again the quarter-final stages eluded Edinburgh.

Realisation of Edinburgh's real potential came later in the season, when after losing twice while the Six Nations was taking place – largely because of the lack of strength in their back-up squad – the club made a late charge with six successive wins, which included two against Cardiff and a crucial away victory over the Ospreys, to clinch second place in the Magners League. Robinson's hands-on coaching could be detected in the improvement of players such as open-side flanker Alan MacDonald, full back Jim Thompson and centre/wing John Houston, all of whom look set to challenge for higher honours in the near future.

Edinburgh parted company with international full back Hugo Southwell, but with Thompson making his mark and Chris Paterson signing up for more, there is no shortage of talent in this position, especially with the arrival from Newcastle Falcons of Scotland A cap Steve Jones. Also away from Edinburgh are hooker Steve Lawrie, who has signed for Doncaster Knights, twice-capped wing Roland Reid, Scotland A centre Calum MacRae, prop Bruce McNeil and Kiwi locks Matt Mustchin and Ben Gissing.

If Edinburgh enjoyed some success, then, judging by the tabular data, it was mediocre business as usual 50 miles to the west, where Glasgow Warriors could finish only seventh in the Magners League while also failing to reach the knockout stages of the Heineken Cup. The overall statistics, however, do not reveal the occasional gems, notably Glasgow's stunning 33-26 Heineken Cup away success against Toulouse, followed a week later by a 13-10 home win against the Dragons. And then there was the 35-31 defeat to Bath at the Rec in a match that revealed the talents of young fly half Ruaridh Jackson, one of three emerging players who could solve Scotland's chronic lack in this position. Jackson, who went on to play for Scotland A in the IRB Nations

BELOW Glasgow's fly half Ruaridh Jackson pictured in action for Scotland A aganst France A in the IRB Nations Cup in Bucharest. Scotland A won the match 22-12 to take the trophy.

FACING PAGE Scrum half A.J. McFarlane is hoisted high as Ayr become Premiership champions after beating Edinburgh Accies 20-10 at Millbrae in March.

PAGE 127 John Houston breaks past Robin Sowden-Taylor during Edinburgh's 16-3 Magners League home win over Cardiff Blues.

Cup in Bucharest, is a product of northeast rugby, having been schooled at Robert Gordon's College in Aberdeen, curiously the same rugby nursery as his half-back partner this season, Chris Cusiter.

Two other young players to come through the Glasgow system were back-row Calum Forrester and lock James Eddie, both of whom won A caps this season. But eclipsing them all last year were the Evans brothers, Thom and Max, whose rapid promotion to the senior Scotland team gave Glasgow a new-found status. The rise of Max Evans meant the demotion of many-times-capped Scotland centre Andy Henderson, who has swapped the glamour of Glasgow for the Gallic mystique of Montauban. Gone, too, are promising back-row Steve Swindall, now part of the Rotherham set-up, Samoan wing Lome Fa'atau, Samoan lock Opeta Palepoi and Scotland-capped scrum half Sam Pinder. In many ways Glasgow have punched above their weight. Their squad is small and shallow in depth compared with many of their big-spending opponents, while their less-than-full-width pitch at Firhill has constrained their ability to play wider rugby.

Although the beneficiaries of a greater share of the Murrayfield purse, Edinburgh, too, look lightweight in terms of investment. That will not change until the money men at Murrayfield reduce further the debt with which the union has been saddled since the rebuilding of the stadium in the early 1990s

and exacerbated by mismanagement of funds during previous regimes.

Taking a cautious approach is all very laudable and in many ways appeals to the Scottish mentality. But the current number of professional players is simply too small to sustain a competitive international team, and without success at the top level, income could begin to diminish, with devastating consequences for the whole of Scottish rugby. Even though it was poorly resourced, the Borders professional team, axed in 2007, still contributed in a major way to the national side. In fact, ten of last season's Scotland squad either started or developed their professional careers with the Borders, a figure that should send a message to Murrayfield's myopic mandarins.

In the absence of a third professional team in Scotland, there is an apparent desire to make the top end of the amateur game semi-professional. Certainly that may have to happen sooner than anticipated following the inclusion of Ayr and Heriot's in the new British & Irish Cup. To some extent Ayr have already gone down the road of semi-professionalism with funds from a backer that allowed the Millbrae club to bring together a squad capable of powering through the Scottish Hydro Electric Premiership to gain a first ever championship title. Critics suggested that Ayr had far too many foreign players in their squad. That may be true, but there was no doubt that the likes of the talented young Taranaki fly half Frazier Climo have raised the bar, and for Scottish rugby that can only be a good thing. Ayr were rarely challenged throughout the season and in the end finished clear winners, losing only three matches in an impressive Premiership campaign.

Arguably the club of the season were Selkirk. The Borders team had expected to struggle in their first season back in the first division, but in the event they made their ground at Philiphaugh a formidable fortress by defeating all the other Premiership teams at home, a record that gave them a well-merited fifth-place finish. If there was the sweet scent of success at Selkirk, then down the road at Hawick there was despair. For the first time in their long and proud history, Hawick felt the pain of relegation, as the Greens, in a year of turmoil, finished bottom of the first division to experience, along with Stirling County, the drop to second-tier rugby. The two demoted clubs exchanged top-flight membership with Dundee HSFP and Stewart's Melville.

The promotion of Stewart's Melville, however, has led to an unhealthy concentration of top rugby in Edinburgh, whose six clubs account for 50 per cent of the first division this season. But with the capital boasting four universities and a number of other tertiary education colleges (in sharp contrast to the Borders), this centralising trend is seemingly unstoppable.

Meanwhile, in the Scottish Hydro Electric Cup it was the turn of Heriot's, the Goldenacre men achieving victory over holders Melrose in the Murrayfield final to reverse the 2008 result; in so doing, they booked their place in the British & Irish Cup. Heriot's, however, in the absence of a strong youth development system at Goldenacre, remain dependent on the plentiful inflow of talent to Edinburgh. Melrose, on the other hand, who have always recruited well on the back of profits from their world famous Sevens event, have now re-established a vibrant youth section that is producing genuinely skilful players. And the coach in charge? None other than J.W. Telfer.

BELOW Heriot's celebrate reversing the previous year's Scottish Hydro Electric Cup final result, having beaten holders Melrose 21-19.

The 1997 Lions tour might have been a different challenge, but Jim Telfer is equally enthusiastic about inspiring a new generation of players at the Greenyards. The future of Melrose, it seems, is now in firm hands. What is needed is this kind of dedication at every club in Scotland. Then, and only then, will Scotland begin to rise again.

Wales: Honours Board
for the Blues   by DAVID STEWART

'After an association with Cardiff Arms Park going back more than a century, home matches will now move to the new Leckwith Stadium, which will be shared with Cardiff City FC'

And about time too! Cardiff Blues have been a team of unfulfilled potential throughout their six-year existence. That frustrating tag was finally shed last season. A stunning 50-12 victory over Gloucester in the EDF Cup final and the narrowest of exits to Leicester in the Heineken semi-finals marked a return to the top table of British Isles and European rugby, where their predecessor club Cardiff once sat so proudly. The tale was less sparkling elsewhere. While the well-resourced Ospreys again underachieved, it was a time of struggle once more for Newport Gwent Dragons and, more troublingly, also this term for Llanelli Scarlets.

As Brian O'Driscoll had pointed out previously, players can ultimately measure their careers by trophies won. By that yardstick the likes of Gethin Jenkins, Martyn Williams, Tom Shanklin and Jamie Roberts can now add club success to a CV that already contains a Grand Slam from the previous year. All had vintage seasons and were rewarded with initial selection for the Lions tour, along with a resurgent Andy Powell and new wunderkind Leigh Halfpenny. Williams seems to mature like a good Bordeaux. Some of his handling, vision and game-awareness in the Twickenham

> **BELOW** Cardiff Blues celebrate their seven-try demolition of Gloucester in the EDF Energy Cup final.

destruction of Gloucester had connoisseurs of those arts thinking they were watching Mike Gibson play at open-side wing forward. That core of Welsh internationals were supplemented by a few canny New Zealanders. Xavier Rush was injured in the early part of the season and ceded the captaincy to Paul Tito, who led by example in all he did. Add the balanced running and goal-kicking of Ben Blair from full back and the trio – along with scrum half Jason Spice – were contributors to a culture that made the Blues winners on good days and tough to beat on the bad ones.

A year earlier they had managed a slightly unexpected quarter-final berth in the Heineken, coming unstuck at Toulouse. This time they roared through the pool phases as top qualifiers, winning six from six, notably at Biarritz (10-6) and Gloucester (16-12), where they only had 14 men for an hour of the game. The victory over Toulouse in the quarter-final, this time at home by 9-6, was the sort of dogged defensive display that head coach Dai Young acknowledged would until latterly have been beyond them. And so to the infamous semi-final against Leicester. A 26-26 tie after extra time led to a place-kicking shoot-out. That the outstanding Martyn Williams should be the player to miss and cost his team a place in the final was cruel indeed. The vast majority of those involved in the sport also now consider that method of deciding a match to be unjust. Hopefully no player will suffer in that way again; it is a different game to soccer.

For the new season, one Blues goal will be greater consistency. A mid-table Magners League position, a long way behind winners Munster, was poor after being runners-up in the two previous campaigns. Changes are afoot. The long-serving Robinson brothers, Jamie and Nicky, are moving on, as is Spice. Gareth Cooper and Sam Norton-Knight from Australia are to be the new halves. And, most poignantly, after an association with Cardiff Arms Park going back more than a century, home matches will now move to the new Leckwith Stadium, which will be shared with Cardiff City FC.

The Ospreys will look back on the season as one of missed opportunity. Fourth place in the Magners, defeat to Gloucester in the semi-finals of their defence of the EDF Cup, and a salutary reverse at Thomond Park (9-43) in the Heineken last eight added up to a frustrating return. Scott Johnson arrived from Australia, via the USA Eagles, in the second half of the season to head up the coaching team previously led on an interim basis by Jon Humphreys and Sean Holley. Many supporters felt this arrangement left a vacuum filled by skipper Ryan Jones, leading to his own loss of form and exclusion from the original Lions selection. The squad contains as much talent as any in Europe. Lee Byrne, Mike Phillips, Shane Williams, Tommy Bowe, Adam Jones and Alun-Wyn Jones were all Test starters with the Lions. Add the oft-injured Gavin Henson and top-class open-side Marty Holah, and it is clear they underperformed, with a lack of onfield harmony plus confused tactics, or at least execution of them, apparent on occasion. Jerry Collins, after an unhappy experience in France, will join the ranks next term.

The western region have already moved to new premises at Parc y Scarlets, their last match at the ancient Stradey being a 27-0 triumph over Bristol in the EDF. A fresh start seems required in terms of their squad, too. Several experienced players, including wing Dafydd James, parted company. Head coach Nigel Davies acknowledges what is needed, 'We have to be committed to home-grown talent'. Bottom of their Heineken pool, failure to qualify in the EDF and fifth in the Magners – these were the milestones marking an ongoing decline in results.

Injuries and contract disputes cast a shadow. Funding threatens to become an issue, with weak crowds at the new ground so far and a surrounding area of neither high population nor strong commerce. Hope is now invested in young players such as lock Dominic Day, centre Nic Reynolds and new caps from Wales's North American venture Jonathan Davies and Daniel Evans. Arrivals are Sean Lamont and prop Rhys Thomas. Much will depend on the steadying influence of Stephen Jones, Matthew Rees and Wallaby David Lyons. A play-off for the last Welsh spot in the Heineken was avoided by encouraging end-of-season wins at Cardiff (30-9) and at home to Ulster (43-17).

Sadly the underfunded Dragons continued their struggles. Paul Turner and his coaching team, with Kiwi skipper Tom Willis, made a little go a fair way, but they still came ninth out of ten teams in the Magners League. They beat Calvisano 42-17 in a play-off, in Italy, to secure their Heineken spot. Again it is their own young players who provide optimism looking ahead. The back-rowers Dan Lydiate and Lewis Evans and full back/fly half Jason Tovey were all original selections for Wales's North American tour. Full back Will Harries of the Welsh Sevens team is a useful acquisition.

You'll be converted

once you see how we go to the ends of earth and beyond to give you the best property advice in Scotland

Culverwell
PROPERTY CONSULTANTS

Ireland: Bragging Rights Secured

by SEAN DIFFLEY

'Not only did Ireland triumph over all opponents, but Leinster defeated all the other club teams in Europe and Munster virtually walked away with the Magners League'

A s for the 2008-09 season, the Irish utterly monopolised 'bragging rights'. It was a case of total superiority in all the major European competitions, the most successful period in the Irish Union's 135-year history.

Sixty-one years earlier, Ireland had won their only other international Grand Slam, in the halcyon days of Karl Mullen and Jack Kyle and all their illustrious colleagues back in 1948. But in 2009 there was a difference from the days of more than half a century ago. This time around, not only did Ireland triumph over all opponents in the Six Nations, but Leinster defeated all the other

club teams in Europe and Munster virtually walked away with the Magners League. It was all quite an accomplishment for a country with one of the smallest rugby populations, completely overshadowed in domestic sport by the numbers involved in Gaelic football, hurling and soccer. But judging by the number of Irish kids, hugely impressed by the rugby success, wearing green jerseys and involving themselves in the game from mini rugby to joining the youth policies of the clubs, rugby is expanding in Ireland.

Ironically, back in 1995 when the famous meeting in Paris opted for professionalism, the Irish were against the proposition but accepted reluctantly. Yet the Irish Rugby Football Union (IRFU) has handled the new era, with all its difficulties, better than most. It has managed to retain the top professional players, eschewing the policies adopted in so many of the other countries of allowing ownership of clubs to be in private hands. Thus the IRFU are the bosses, the employers, the paymasters, and have escaped the problems encountered by other national unions who are dictated to by avaricious and wealthy owners.

So recent successes at most levels, culminating in last season's Grand Slam and Heineken Cup triumphs, did not come about by accident. Irish rugby, it is hardly necessary to say, has it problems, such as accommodating the 16 senior clubs that make up the first division of the AIB All Ireland League – clubs like Shannon, Cork Constitution and Ballymena – who feel neglected compared with the senior professional provinces. But overall the Irish game is healthy and interest is sky-high, as demonstrated by the record attendance of over 80,000 for the Leinster v Munster Heineken Cup semi-final at Croke Park.

The 2008-09 Leinster-Munster saga was fascinating. Munster were nearly everybody's forecast for another Heineken success and underlined that with a 22-5 Magners League victory over Leinster at Thomond Park in April. Leinster were proving a strange lot. They had a host of star world-class players like Brian O'Driscoll, but over the seasons the province were, to their supporters, infuriatingly inconsistent; and even when they beat Harlequins 6-5 in the Heineken quarter-finals away, they were not fancied against Munster in the semis. Every pundit, every newspaper correspondent tipped Munster to win at Croke Park. After all, there was Munster's great tradition in the competition, and they had such stalwarts as Paul O'Connell and the match-winning skills of such as Ronan O'Gara.

Yet to some amazement, Leinster utterly overwhelmed Munster in almost every sector. O'Gara was swamped, his pack were completely dominated and Leinster were decisive winners. Rocky Elsom, their Australian flanker, played a blinder. Unfortunately for Leinster, though, the Australian Rugby Union insisted that if Elsom wanted to play Test rugby for the Wallabies he would have to return to Australia and turn out for a home side. Leinster made no secret of their efforts to retain Elsom – surely one of the world's greatest flankers – but though Rocky would have liked to continue next season with Leinster, his preferred ambition was to play for Australia.

Leinster owe a lot to their Aussie coach Michael Cheika, who has Alan Gaffney assisting with the backs coaching, but his preference for Felipe Contepomi meant that young Johnny Sexton, the reserve fly half, spent most of the season on the bench. Then, for the Heineken Cup final against Leicester, the Argentinian was injured and unavailable, and Sexton, virtually unproved, was drafted into the side. He had a splendid game, and in a fairy-tale ending kicked the penalty goal that sealed victory. Furthermore, Sexton's competitive zeal and coolness under pressure, his line kicking as well

Because every project presents unique demands, we work closely with clients to understand their objectives. We offer in-depth industry knowledge, delivering practical solutions and clear strategies aimed at making the deal work.

With commitment and innovation "clients are impressed with the team's level of creativity".†

With an integrated network of leading individuals, Clifford Chance's International Real Estate Group has the commitment, resources and know-how to get deals done, whatever and wherever they are.

For more information please visit **www.cliffordchance.com/real estate**

† Chambers & Partners Europe 2007

C L I F F O R D
C H A N C E

as his penalty kicking all seemed to solve an Irish puzzle. Ronan O'Gara cannot go on forever, and where on earth were Ireland to find an adequate replacement? After Sexton's accomplished Heineken final display, the consensus was that he could prove to be the heir apparent.

So Irish sides have now won the Heineken Cup in two successive seasons. Ulster, of course, won at Lansdowne Road in 1999, but affairs are not running smoothly nowadays. Matt Williams, formerly the Leinster coach, seemed to be building a young Ulster side into a team that could improve matters, but at the end of the season he resigned suddenly for domestic reasons and returned to Australia. As I write, his replacement hasn't been named yet, but Jeremy Davidson, late of Castres and already Ulster forwards coach, is being widely mentioned. Connacht are still the 'Cinderella' side and not too surprisingly finished at the bottom of the Magners.

The AIB All Ireland League had Shannon defeating Garryowen and Clontarf beating Cork Constitution in the top clubs' semi-finals. The final between Shannon and Clontarf ended all-square, 19-19, after extra time, and the issue was eventually decided not by a series of penalty kicks but on the basis of who had scored the first try, the sides having registered two apiece. David O'Donovan had crossed first for Shannon on 23 minutes, and the Limerick club were therefore awarded the title. The matter caused a lot of vigorous debate, and the consensus was that a replay would have been the correct way forward. But Shannon didn't object too much. They had won the league again.

At junior club level, Ballynahinch, a small club from Co. Down, had a remarkable season. They dominated the junior ranks in Ulster, won the second division of the AIB All Ireland League and then in regal fashion beat Cork Constitution's senior side 17-6 in the final of the AIB Cup. And Con were Munster Senior Cup winners for the season. We'll be hearing a lot more about Ballynahinch, surely the club team of the year.

France: Catalans Grab Championship
by CHRIS THAU

'But then the canny Catalans, who had been expecting the onslaught, had prepared an ambush for the Clermont forwards. The bait was going to be their notoriously suspect scrummage'

Even by the high operatic standards of French rugby, this was a season of tremendous domestic and international drama. It started with Toulouse being knocked out in the quarter-finals of the Heineken Cup, an unusual occurrence for the 'Rolls-Royce' of French club rugby, used to reaching finals and winning gold medals. A few weeks later, Toulouse ended their wretched season with a 19-9 defeat at the hands of Clermont in the semi-finals of the Top 14, while in the other semi-final the underachievers from Perpignan put Parisian frontrunners Stade Français to the sword 25-21 to set up the first ever Perpignan v Clermont final in the history of the championship.

After that, nothing seemed to be the same at the two clubs who between them have dominated French rugby for the past decade. After the four-point semi-final defeat, the touch of the Parisian Maecenas Max Guazzini was questioned, coach Fabrice Landreau announced that he was heading for greener pastures and head coach Ewen McKenzie seemed to be trying to justify himself to the expectant media when he explained why his men lost the match. Similarly at Toulouse the talismanic Byron Kelleher looked pedestrian and out of sync, the farewell of Fabien Pelous after 16 years and 118 international selections turned into a fairly sad affair and all of a sudden the all-conquering head coach Guy Novès, after the eighteenth semi-final of his coaching career, seemed vulnerable.

Events at the relegation end of the division added to the sense of drama, with Toulon, inspired by a rejuvenated Tana Umaga defying his biological age (35), defeating a lethargic Dax 22-12 to retain their Top 14 status, which in turn sent Thomas Lièvremont's men into the second division. Similarly, another struggling giant, Bourgoin, managed to defeat Castres by 31 points to 23, which preserved their Top 14 status but had a knock-on effect on struggling Mont-de-Marsan, who were relegated. It is perhaps of interest that the two relegated clubs had the smallest budgets in the Top 14.

The Top 14 final provided a brief return to reality, although the way Perpignan transformed their set scrum – perceived to be their Achilles' heel – into an area of contest and ambiguity was nothing short of a miracle. Their head coach, Jacques Brunel, though, the former French assistant coach under Bernard Laporte, would argue that a miracle in rugby is a product of sound preparation and quality decision-making. Interestingly, this was Clermont's third consecutive final, their tenth overall, and Vernon Cotter, the outstanding Kiwi coach who transformed the Michelin club into genuine Top 14 title contenders, must have hoped that this was going to be their 'third time lucky'. Indeed, such was their control of the game in the early stages of the first half that after Napolioni Nalaga's try in the 10th minute it looked as though they were going to turn the tables on Perpignan.

But then the canny Catalans, who had been expecting the onslaught, had prepared an ambush for the Clermont forwards. The bait was going to be their notoriously suspect scrummage. This is why some five minutes after Nalaga's try, at a scrum in the vicinity of Clermont's 22, Perpignan tight-head prop and skipper Nicolas Mas warned his multinational front-row partners, Englishman Perry Freshwater and Romanian Marius Tincu, that the time had come to implement what they had been rehearsing for some time – that was challenge up front the Clermont scrum, weakened at that stage by the injury to Martín Scelzo earlier in the game. It was as audacious as it was sensible. If there was a moment when the formidable Clermont scrummage was vulnerable, it was then, before Scelzo was replaced. The astonishing vision of the Clermont scrum being shunted backwards was a sight to behold and was instantly rewarded with a penalty, duly converted by young full back Jérôme Porical.

Some ten minutes later, when Scelzo's replacement Davit Zirakashvili attempted to re-establish the 'original order' up front, a violent altercation between the two hookers, Tincu and Mario

Ledesma, ended in an all-out brawl that took the sting out of Clermont. Although Clermont led 10-6 at half-time and played, on occasions, sublime rugby, they failed again in their quest for the legendary Bouclier de Brennus. Symbolically, the hero of the hour was full back Porical – grandson of Paul Porical, a champion with Perpignan in 1938 – who was watched by his father Gérald, a finalist with Perpignan in 1977. Porical recorded an impeccable five out of five kicks at goal, while a dropped goal by Gavin Hume and a try by David Marty completed Perpignan's 22-point tally. Clermont's 13 points consisted of Nalaga's try plus two penalties and a conversion from Brock James.

The following weekend the French team, coached by Marc Lièvremont and Emile Ntamack, defeated New Zealand 27-22 in a Test of unreal drama in Dunedin. The manner of the win, with the French playing imperial rugby, as an inspired TV reporter described it, was perhaps as significant as the win itself, the first for France in New Zealand since 1994 and only the fourth French victory since they have been touring the country. France lost the second Test just 14-10 to share the series, but the matches took such a physical and emotional toll on top of a long and exhausting season that the French were beaten 22-6 by Australia a week later.

BELOW Perpignan enjoy their moment of glory after defeating Clermont-Auvergne 22-13 in the Top 14 final to get their hands on the Bouclier de Brennus.

Italy: Champions in the Wilderness?

by CHRIS THAU

'Unless a miracle happens between now and next year when two Italian teams are expected to join the Magners League, Treviso are unlikely to be one of them'

Although Montepaschi Viadana finished the Italian Super 10 at the top of the league, runners-up Benetton Treviso managed to turn the tables on their arch-rivals, winning the Italian Championship final 29-20 at the Flaminio Stadium in Rome to secure their fourteenth title in their 57-year history. Last year's champion club, Cammi Calvisano, finished third and were knocked out 28-24 on aggregate by Treviso in the semi-finals, winning the home leg 18-13 but losing the away clash 6-15.

In the other semi-final, Viadana prevailed over fourth-placed Femi CZ Rovigo in both matches, winning 23-19 away and 15-11 at home. The final was an exciting occasion, with Treviso, coached by Franco Smith, scoring four tries to two touchdowns by Jim Love's Viadana, in a match played at high pace and intensity. The reliable Viadana full back Garry Law was the game's top scorer with 15 points (one try, two penalties and two conversions), though Benetton's long-serving outside half, Marius Goosen, was right behind him with 14 (one try, one penalty and three conversions).

But the celebrations of the winning team had a hollow ring to them. For reasons unknown, Treviso do not feature highly in the long-term plans of the Italian Federation. Unless a miracle happens between now and next year when two Italian teams are expected to join the Magners League, Treviso are unlikely to be one of them, which must be upsetting. It has been reliably reported that one of the two teams – in fact regional selections – will come from Rome, under the name of Praetorians, and the other from Parma, called Aironi, leaving Veneto, historically the most productive Italian rugby nursery, and its leading club Treviso out in the wilderness. It is, however, likely that Treviso will be able to carry on playing in the Heineken Cup; but deprived of the right competitive framework, their chances of making a breakthrough against formidable opponents appear minimal.

Similarly Brescia rugby, with its leading club Calvisano, who together with Treviso and Viadana dominated the Italian rugby scene with great authority for more than a decade, has been ignored, which would have meant that Calvisano would only play Italian Super 10 and European Challenge Cup rugby. Apparently all this annoyed the powerful president of Calvisano, Alfredo Gavazzi, a former vice-president of the Italian Federation, so much that he decided to pull the club out of the Super 10 and return to amateur status, making all his professional staff redundant. The shake-up at the top of the Italian league has had an unexpected side effect at the bottom end of it. The decision to pull Calvisano out has allowed in the loser of the Super 10 promotion play-offs, the club from L'Aquila, very much in the news during the spring.

The town of L'Aquila, the capital of the Abruzzo region, east of Rome, was hit by a powerful earthquake, measuring 6.3 on the Richter scale, Italy's worst for 300 years. Several hundred people died, including promising rugby player Lorenzo Sebastian, a member of the National Academy and an Italy Under 20 international. The players, while mourning his death, played a leading role in the rescue operation, and the rugby field became a shelter for the many families left without a roof over their heads. The L'Aquila club, formed in 1936, was one of the leading Italian clubs during the amateur days, when they won the national championship five times and were famous for their dynamic style and quality players, including the legendary Serafino Ghizzoni, Massimo Mascioletti and Luigi Troiani.

According to Italian sources, all this commotion in Italian rugby is designed to enable the federation to control the selection of the two regional sides – for whom mostly (or only) players eligible to play for Italy will be selected. Strengthening the elite end of the Italian domestic game, by increasing the number of quality players eligible for selection, is a priority demanded with insistence by Italy coach Nick Mallett. At the development end of Italian rugby, former national coach Georges Coste is doing a sterling job, producing talented players year after year. But that is not enough. The clubs employ too many foreign players, which has a direct impact on national team selection. Italy have lost 11 matches on the trot since 8 November 2008, and although Mallett's position is not under immediate threat, he needs to start winning if he wishes to retain his credibility with his employer and the increasingly vocal Italian media.

Before the summer tour to the southern hemisphere, Mallett was running in circles trying to find suitable players to replace the cohorts of injured regulars unable to play. He pulled nearly ten players from the Italy A squad, preparing for the IRB Nations Cup in Bucharest, to make up the numbers in his squad heading Down Under. By far the best find was former Australian rugby league star Craig Gower, who has an Italian passport and plays his rugby for Bayonne in the French Top 14. Gower has added the missing dimension to Italian back play, as well as a bit of backbone and realism. As a result Italy, although they lost all three Tests in Australia and New Zealand, gave a good account of themselves, which provides some hope for the future. Gower, who is in his early thirties, should be available for RWC 2011, when all Mallett's work will be scrutinised and measured.

BELOW Benetton Treviso's fly half Marius Goosen, supported by Michael Horak (now of Saracens), beats Charlie Hore's tackle during the Super 10 final in Rome. Goosen contributed 14 points to his side's victory.

A Summary of the Season 2008-09

by TERRY COOPER

INTERNATIONAL RUGBY

BRITISH & IRISH LIONS TO SOUTH AFRICA
JUNE/JULY 2009

Opponents	Results
Royal XV	W 37-25
Golden Lions	W 74-10
Free State Cheetahs	W 26-24
Natal Sharks	W 39-3
Western Province	W 26-23
Southern Kings	W 20-8
SOUTH AFRICA	L 21-26
Emerging Springboks	D 13-13
SOUTH AFRICA	L 25-28
SOUTH AFRICA	W 28-9

Played 10 Won 7 Drawn 1 Lost 2

AUSTRALIA TO EUROPE
NOVEMBER 2008

Opponents	Results
ITALY	W 30-20
ENGLAND	W 28-14
FRANCE	W 18-13
WALES	L 18-21
Barbarians	W 18-11

Played 5 Won 4 Lost 1

NEW ZEALAND TO BRITISH ISLES
NOVEMBER 2008

Opponents	Results
SCOTLAND	W 32-6
IRELAND	W 22-3
Munster	W 18-16
WALES	W 29-9
ENGLAND	W 32-6

Played 5 Won 5

SOUTH AFRICA TO UNITED KINGDOM
NOVEMBER 2008

Opponents	Results
WALES	W 20-15
SCOTLAND	W 14-10
ENGLAND	W 42- 6

Played 3 Won 3

PACIFIC ISLANDS TO EUROPE
NOVEMBER 2008

Opponents	Results
ENGLAND	L 13-39
FRANCE	L 17-42
ITALY	W 25-17

Played 3 Won 1 Lost 2

ARGENTINA TO EUROPE
NOVEMBER 2008

Opponents	Results
FRANCE	L 6-12
ITALY	W 22-14
IRELAND	L 3-17

Played 3 Won 1 Lost 2

CANADA TO EUROPE
NOVEMBER 2008

Opponents	Results
PORTUGAL	W 21-13
IRELAND	L 0-55
WALES	L 13-34
SCOTLAND	L 0-41

Played 4 Won 1 Lost 3

ENGLAND V ARGENTINA
JUNE 2009

(Held in England & Argentina)

Opponents	Results
ARGENTINA	W 37-15
ARGENTINA	L 22-24

Played 2 Won 1 Lost 1

IRELAND TO NORTH AMERICA
JUNE 2009

Opponents	Results
CANADA	W 25-6
USA	W 27-10

Played 2 Won 2

WALES TO NORTH AMERICA
JUNE 2009

Opponents	Results
CANADA	W 32-23
USA	W 48-15

Played 2 Won 2

FRANCE TO NEW ZEALAND & AUSTRALIA
JUNE 2009

Opponents	Results
NEW ZEALAND	W 27-22
NEW ZEALAND	L 10-14
AUSTRALIA	L 6-22

Played 3 Won 1 Lost 2

ITALY TO AUSTRALIA & NEW ZEALAND
JUNE 2009

Opponents	Results
AUSTRALIA	L 8-31
AUSTRALIA	L 12-34
NEW ZEALAND	L 6-27

Played 3 Lost 3

ROYAL BANK OF SCOTLAND
SIX NATIONS CHAMPIONSHIP 2009

Results

England	36	Italy	11
Ireland	30	France	21
Scotland	13	Wales	26
France	22	Scotland	13
Wales	23	England	15
Italy	9	Ireland	38
France	21	Wales	16
Scotland	26	Italy	6
Ireland	14	England	13
Italy	15	Wales	20
Scotland	15	Ireland	22
England	34	France	10
Italy	8	France	50
England	26	Scotland	12
Wales	15	Ireland	17

Final table

	P	W	D	L	F	A	PD	Pts
Ireland	5	5	0	0	121	73	48	10
England	5	3	0	2	124	70	54	6
France	5	3	0	2	124	101	23	6
Wales	5	3	0	2	100	81	19	6
Scotland	5	1	0	4	79	102	-23	2
Italy	5	0	0	5	49	170	-121	0

UNDER 20 SIX NATIONS 2009

Results

Scotland	18	Wales	17
Ireland	9	France	6
England	17	Italy	0

France	30	Scotland	3
Wales	16	England	28
Italy	23	Ireland	29
Ireland	19	England	18
Scotland	14	Italy	10
France	40	Wales	20
Scotland	35	Ireland	20
England	11	France	31
Italy	14	Wales	34
Italy	10	France	43
Wales	6	Ireland	9
England	20	Scotland	6

Final table

	P	W	D	L	F	A	PD	Pts
France	5	4	0	1	150	53	97	8
Ireland	5	4	0	1	86	88	-2	8
England	5	3	0	2	94	72	22	6
Scotland	5	3	0	2	76	97	-21	6
Wales	5	1	0	4	93	109	-16	2
Italy	5	0	0	5	57	137	-80	0

WOMEN'S SIX NATIONS 2009

Results

Ireland	7	France	5
England	69	Italy	13
Scotland	10	Wales	31
Wales	16	England	15
Italy	17	Ireland	35
France	25	Scotland	12
Ireland	13	England	29
Scotland	13	Italy	10
France	27	Wales	5
Scotland	0	Ireland	23
England	52	France	7
Italy	7	Wales	29
Wales	13	Ireland	10
England	72	Scotland	3
Italy	10	France	14

Final table

	P	W	D	L	F	A	PD	Pts
England	5	4	0	1	237	52	185	8
Wales	5	4	0	1	94	69	25	8
Ireland	5	3	0	2	88	64	24	6
France	5	3	0	2	78	86	-8	6
Scotland	5	1	0	4	38	161	-123	2
Italy	5	0	0	5	57	160	-103	0

UNDER 18 SIX NATIONS FESTIVAL 2009

(Held in April in Italy. Incomplete as France withdrew and the England v Ireland match was cancelled)

Results of matches played

Wales	15	Ireland	22
Italy	3	England	61
Italy	3	Ireland	29
England	75	Scotland	0
Wales	23	Scotland	13

PRIORITY

O₂ customers get priority treatment at Twickenham on match days

Text ENGLAND to 62002

We're better, connected

TRI-NATIONS 2008

Results

New Zealand	19	South Africa	8
New Zealand	28	South Africa	30
Australia	16	South Africa	9
Australia	34	New Zealand	19
New Zealand	39	Australia	10
South Africa	0	New Zealand	19
South Africa	15	Australia	27
South Africa	53	Australia	8
Australia	24	New Zealand	28

Champions: New Zealand

TRI-NATIONS 2009 (to date)

Results

New Zealand	22	Australia	16
South Africa	28	New Zealand	19
South Africa	31	New Zealand	19
South Africa	29	Australia	17
Australia	18	New Zealand	19
Australia	25	South Africa	32
Australia	21	South Africa	6
New Zealand		South Africa	
New Zealand		Australia	

IRB PACIFIC NATIONS CUP 2009

Results

Samoa	16	Junior All Blacks	17
Tonga	22	Fiji	36
Japan	15	Samoa	34
Junior All Blacks	45	Fiji	17
Samoa	27	Tonga	13
Japan	21	Junior All Blacks	52
Tonga	19	Japan	21
Samoa	14	Fiji	19
Tonga	25	Junior All Blacks	47
Fiji	40	Japan	39

Champions: Junior All Blacks

CHURCHILL CUP 2009

(Held in June in Denver, USA)

Pool matches

Argentina Jaguars	20	England Saxons	28
Georgia	10	Canada	42
Argentina Jaguars	35	USA	14
Ireland A	30	Canada	19
Ireland A	40	Georgia	5
England Saxons	56	USA	17

Bowl Final

USA	31	Georgia	13

Plate Final

Argentina Jaguars	44	Canada	29

Cup Final

Ireland A	49	England Saxons	22

IRB NATIONS CUP 2009

(Held in June in Bucharest, Romania)

Italy A	15	France A	31
Scotland A	49	Russia	7
Uruguay	11	Romania	17
Scotland A	27	Uruguay	3
Italy A	35	Russia	3
France A	20	Romania	16
Russia	29	Uruguay	26
Italy A	24	Romania	13
France A	12	Scotland A	22

Winners: Scotland A

IRB JUNIOR WORLD CHAMPIONSHIP 2009

(Held in June in Japan)

Semi-finals

New Zealand	31	Australia	17
South Africa	21	England	40

Final

New Zealand	44	England	28

RWC SEVENS 2009

(Held in March in Dubai)

Bowl Final

Zimbabwe	17	Ireland	14

Plate Final

Australia	17	Scotland	21

Cup Final

Wales	19	Argentina	12

Women's Cup Final

New Zealand	10	Australia	15

IRB SEVENS WORLD SERIES FINALS 2008-09

Dubai

South Africa	19	England	12

South Africa (George)

South Africa	12	New Zealand	7

New Zealand (Wellington)

England	19	New Zealand	17

United States (San Diego)

Argentina	19	England	14

Hong Kong

Fiji	26	South Africa	24

Australia (Adelaide)

South Africa	26	Kenya	7

England (Twickenham)

England	31	New Zealand	26

Scotland (Murrayfield)

Fiji	20	South Africa	19

IRB Sevens Champions: South Africa

SCOTLAND'S FINEST FLY HALF.

PREVIEW OF THE SEASON 2009-10

Key Players
selected by IAN ROBERTSON

IRELAND

JAMIE HEASLIP
Leinster, Ireland and Lions
Height: 6ft 4ins Weight: 17st 7lbs
No. 8 – 21 caps
1st cap v Pacific Islanders 2006
Lions Tests (3) v South Africa 2009

ROB KEARNEY
Leinster, Ireland and Lions
Height: 6ft 1in Weight: 14st

Full back – 19 caps
1st cap v Argentina 2007
Lions Tests (3) v South Africa 2009

ENGLAND

TOM CROFT
Leicester, England and Lions
Height: 6ft 6ins Weight: 16st 7lbs
Flanker – 13 caps
1st cap v France 2008
Lions Tests (3) v South Africa 2009

UGO MONYE
Harlequins, England and Lions
Height: 6ft 2ins Weight: 14st 13lbs
Wing – 6 caps
1st cap v Pacific Islanders 2008
Lions Tests (2) v South Africa 2009

FRANCE

SYLVAIN MARCONNET
Stade Français and France
Height: 6ft Weight: 17st 7lbs
Prop – 76 caps
1st cap v Argentina 1998

FRANCOIS TRINH-DUC
Montpellier and France
Height: 6ft 1in Weight: 13st 5lbs
Fly half – 12 caps
1st cap v Scotland 2008

Six Nations Championship
2009-10

WALES

MATTHEW REES

Scarlets, Wales and Lions
Height: 6ft 2ins Weight: 17st
Hooker – 33 caps
1st cap v USA 2005
Lions Tests (3) v South Africa 2009

JAMIE ROBERTS

Cardiff Blues, Wales and Lions
Height: 6ft 4ins Weight: 16st 3lbs
Centre – 14 caps
1st cap v Scotland 2008
Lions Tests (2) v South Africa 2009

SCOTLAND

NATHAN HINES

Perpignan, Scotland and Lions
Height: 6ft 7ins Weight: 17st 6lbs
Lock – 58 caps
1st cap v New Zealand 2000
Lions tour to South Africa 2009

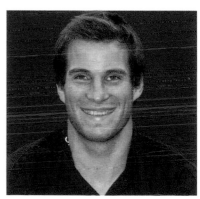

PHIL GODMAN

Edinburgh and Scotland
Height: 5ft 10ins Weight: 14st
Fly half – 17 caps
1st cap v Romania 2005

ITALY

LEONARDO GHIRALDINI

Calvisano and Italy
Height: 6ft Weight: 15st 5lbs
Hooker – 21 caps
1st cap v Japan 2006

CRAIG GOWER

Bayonne and Italy
(ex-Australian RL international)
Height: 5ft 9ins Weight: 14st 1lb
Fly half – 3 caps
1st cap v Australia 2009

Fixtures 2009-10

AUGUST 2009

Sat. 29th — AUSTRALIA v S AFRICA
(Tri-Nations)
Scottish Hydro Prem/ship 1-3
Scottish Hydro Nat. Lges 1-3
Welsh Principality Premiership

SEPTEMBER 2009

Fri. 4th to — Guinness English Premiership
Sun. 6th — Magners Celtic League (1)
English National Championship
Sat. 5th — AUSTRALIA v S AFRICA
(Tri-Nations)
English Nat. Lges 1, 2N & S
Scottish Hydro Prem/ship 1-3
Scottish Hydro Nat. Lges 1-3
Welsh Principality Premiership
Swalec Welsh Nat. Lges E, W, N
Mon. 7th — Guinness 'A' League
Fri. 11th to — Guinness English Premiership
Sun. 13th — Magners Celtic League (2)
English National Championship
Sat. 12th — NEW ZEALAND v S AFRICA
(Tri-Nations)
English Nat. Lges 1, 2N & S
Scottish Hydro Prem/ship 1-3
Scottish Hydro Nat. Lges 1-3
Welsh Principality Premiership
Swalec Welsh Nat. Lges E, W, N
Mon. 14th — Guinness 'A' League
Fri. 18th and — Magners Celtic League (3)
Sat. 19th — Welsh Principality Premiership
Fri.18th to — Guinness English Premiership
Sun. 20th — English National Championship
Sat. 19th — NEW ZEALAND v AUSTRALIA
(Tri-Nations)
English Nat. Lges 1, 2N & S
Scottish Hydro Prem/ship 1-3
Scottish Hydro Nat. Lges 1-3
Swalec Welsh Nat. Lges E, W, N
Tue. 22nd — Welsh Principality Premiership
Fri. 25th to — Guinness English Premiership
Sun. 27th — Magners Celtic League (4)
Sat. 26th — English Nat. Lges 1, 2N & S
Scottish Hydro Prem/ship 1-3
Scottish Hydro Nat. Lges 1-3
Welsh Principality Premiership
Swalec Welsh Nat. Lges E, W, N
AIB Irish Cup (1)
Sat. 26th and
Sun. 27th — English National Championship

OCTOBER 2009

Fri. 2nd to — Guinness English Premiership
Sun. 4th — English National Championship
Magners Celtic League (5)
Sat. 3rd — English Nat. Lges 1, 2N & S

Scottish Hydro Prem/ship 1-3
Scottish Hydro Nat. Lges 1-3
Welsh Principality Premiership
Swalec Welsh Nat. Lges E, W, N
AIB Irish Leagues
Mon. 5th — Guinness 'A' League
Thu. 8th to
Sun. 11th — European Challenge Cup (1)
Fri. 9th and
Sat. 10th — English Nat. Lge 2N
Fri. 9th to — Heineken Cup (1)
Sun. 11th — English National Championship
Sat. 10th — English Nat. Lges 1, 2S
Scottish Hydro Prem/ship 1-3
Scottish Hydro Nat. Lges 1-3
Welsh Principality Premiership
Swalec Welsh Nat. Lges E, W, N
Swalec Bowl (1)
AIB Irish Leagues
Thu. 15th to
Sun. 18th — European Challenge Cup (2)
Fri. 16th and
Sat. 17th — English National Championship
Fri. 16th to
Sun. 18th — Heineken Cup (2)
Sat. 17th — English Nat. Lges 1, 2N & S
Scottish Hydro Prem/ship 1-3
Scottish Hydro Nat. Lges 1-3
Welsh Principality Premiership
Swalec Welsh Nat. Lges E, W, N
AIB Irish Cup (2)
Fri. 23rd and
Sat. 24th — Magners Celtic League (6)
Fri. 23rd to
Sun. 25th — English National Championship
Sat. 24th — English Nat. Lges 1, 2N & S
Scottish Hydro Prem/ship 1-3
Scottish Hydro Nat. Lges 1-3
Welsh Principality Premiership
Swalec Welsh Nat. Lges E, W, N
AIB Irish Leagues
Sat. 24th and
Sun. 25th — Guinness English Premiership
Mon. 26th — Guinness 'A' League
Fri. 30th to — Guinness English Premiership
Sun. 1st Nov. — Magners Celtic League (7)
Sat. 31st — NEW ZEALAND v AUSTRALIA
(Japan)
English National Championship
English Nat. Lges 1, 2N & S
Scottish Hydro Prem/ship 1-3
Scottish Hydro Nat. Lges 1-3
Welsh Principality Premiership
Swalec Welsh Nat. Lges E, W
Swalec Plate (1)
Swalec Bowl (2)
AIB Irish Leagues

NOVEMBER 2009

Fri. 6th to	English National Championship
Sun. 8th	Anglo-Welsh Cup (1)
Sat. 7th	ENGLAND v AUSTRALIA
	WALES v NEW ZEALAND
	English Nat. Lges 1, 2N & S
	Scottish Hydro Prem/ship 1-3
	Scottish Hydro Nat. Lges 1-3
	Welsh Principality Premiership
	AIB Irish Cup (3)
Fri. 13th	WALES v SAMOA
Sat. 14th	ENGLAND v ARGENTINA
	SCOTLAND v FIJI
	FRANCE v SOUTH AFRICA
	ITALY v NEW ZEALAND
	English National Championship
	English Nat. Lges 1, 2N & S
	Anglo-Welsh Cup (2)
	Scottish Hydro Prem/ship 1-3
	Scottish Hydro Nat. Lges 1-3
	Welsh Principality Premiership
	Swalec Welsh Nat. Lges E, W, N
	Swalec Cup (1)
	Swalec Plate (2)
	Swalec Bowl (3)
	AIB Irish Leagues
Sun. 15th	IRELAND v AUSTRALIA
Fri. 20th to	
Sun. 22nd	British & Irish Cup (1)
Sat. 21st	ENGLAND v NEW ZEALAND
	WALES v ARGENTINA
	SCOTLAND v AUSTRALIA
	IRELAND v FIJI
	FRANCE v SAMOA
	ITALY v SOUTH AFRICA
	AIB Irish Cup quarter-finals
Sat. 21st and	
Sun. 22nd	Guinness English Premiership
Fri. 27th and	
Sat. 28th	Guinness English Premiership
Fri. 27th to	
Sun 29th	British & Irish Cup (2)
Sat. 28th	WALES v AUSTRALIA
	IRELAND v SOUTH AFRICA
	SCOTLAND v ARGENTINA
	FRANCE v NEW ZEALAND
	English Nat. Lges 1, 2N & S
	Scottish Hydro Prem/ship 1-3
	Scottish Hydro Nat. Lges 1-3
	Scottish Hydro Regional Bowl (1)

DECEMBER 2009

Fri. 4th and	
Sat. 5th	English National Championship
Fri. 4th to	
Sun. 6th	Magners Celtic League (8)
Sat. 5th	Barbarians v New Zealand
	English Nat. Lges 1, 2N & S
	Scottish Hydro Prem/ship 1-3
	Scottish Hydro Nat. Lges 1-3
	Welsh Principality Premiership
	Swalec Welsh Nat. Lges E, W, N
	AIB Irish Leagues
Sat. 5th and	
Sun. 6th	Guinness English Premiership
Mon. 7th	Guinness 'A' League
Thu. 10th	Oxford U v Cambridge U (Twickenham)
Thu. 10th to	
Sat. 12th	European Challenge Cup (3)
Fri. 11th to	
Sun. 13th	Heineken Cup (3)
Sat. 12th	English Nat. Lges 1, 2N & S
	Scottish Hydro Prem/ship 1-3
	Scottish Hydro Nat. Lges 1-3
	Welsh Principality Premiership
	AIB Irish Leagues
Sat. 12th and	
Sun. 13th	English National Championship
Thu. 17th to	
Sun. 20th	European Challenge Cup (4)
Fri. 18th and	
Sat. 19th	English National Championship
Fri. 18th to	
Sun. 20th	Heineken Cup (4)
Sat. 19th	English Nat. Lges 1, 2N & S
	Scottish Hydro Prem/ship 1-3
	Scottish Hydro Nat. Lges 1-3
	Welsh Principality Premiership
	AIB Irish Cup semi-finals
Sat. 26th	English Nat. Lge 1
	Welsh Principality Premiership
	Swalec Welsh Nat. Lges E, W
Sat. 26th and	Guinness English Premiership
Sun 27th	English National Championship
	Magners Celtic League (9)
Thu. 31st to	
Sun. 3rd Jan	Magners Celtic League (10)

JANUARY 2010

Fri. 1st to	
Sun. 3rd	Guinness English Premiership
Sat. 2nd	English Nat. Lges 1, 2N & S
	Welsh Principality Premiership
	Swalec Welsh Nat. Lges E, W
Sat. 2nd and	
Sun. 3rd	English National Championship
Mon. 4th	Guinness 'A' League
Fri. 8th	Magners Celtic League (11)
Fri. 8th to	
Sun. 10th	Guinness English Premiership
Sat. 9th	English Nat. Lges 1, 2N & S
	Scottish Hydro Prem/ship 1-3
	Scottish Hydro Nat. Lges 1-3
	Welsh Principality Premiership
	Swalec Welsh Nat. Lges E, W, N
	AIB Irish Leagues
Sat. 9th and	
Sun. 10th	English National Championship
Mon. 11th	Guinness 'A' League
Thu. 14th to	
Sun. 17th	European Challenge Cup (5)

Fri. 15th to			Swalec Cup (3)
Sun. 17th	Heineken Cup (5)		Swalec Plate (4)
Sat. 16th	English National Championship		Swalec Bowl (5)
	English Nat. Lges 1, 2N & S		AIB Irish Leagues
	Scottish Hydro Prem/ship 1-3	Fri. 26th	WALES v FRANCE (8pm)
	Scottish Hydro Nat. Lges 1-3	Fri. 26th to	
	Welsh Principality Premiership	Sun. 28th	Guinness English Premiership
	Swalec Welsh Nat. Lges E, W		British & Irish Cup (4)
	Swalec Cup (2)	Sat. 27th	ITALY v SCOTLAND (2.30pm)
	Swalec Plate (3)		ENGLAND v IRELAND (4pm)
	Swalec Bowl (4)		English Nat. Lges 1, 2N & S
	AIB Irish Leagues		Welsh Principality Premiership

Thu. 21st to		
Sun. 24th	European Challenge Cup (6)	**MARCH 2010**
Fri. 22nd to		Fri. 5th	Magners Celtic League (13)
Sun. 24th	Heineken Cup (6)	Fri. 5th to	
Sat. 23rd	English Nat. Lges 1, 2N & S	Sun. 7th	Guinness English Premiership
	Scottish Hydro Prem/ship 1-3		British & Irish Cup (5)
	Scottish Hydro Nat. Lges 1-3	Sat. 6th	English Nat. Lges 1, 2N & S
	Welsh Principality Premiership		Scottish Hydro Prem/ship 1-3
	Swalec Welsh Nat. Lges E, W, N		Scottish Hydro Nat. Lges 1-3
	AIB Irish Leagues		Scottish Hydro Regional Bowl (3)
Sat. 23rd and			Welsh Principality Premiership
Sun. 24th	English National Championship		Swalec Welsh Nat. Lges E, W
Sat. 30th	English National Championship		AIB Irish Leagues
	English Nat. Lges 1, 2N & S	Sat. 13th	IRELAND v WALES (2.30pm)
	Anglo-Welsh Cup (3)		SCOTLAND v ENGLAND (5pm)
	Scottish Hydro Prem/ship 1-3		English Nat. Lge 1
	Scottish Hydro Nat. Lges 1-3		Scottish Hydro Premier Cup (2)
	Welsh Principality Premiership		Scottish Hydro Nat. Shield (2)
	Swalec Welsh Nat. Lges E, W, N		Welsh Principality Premiership
	AIB Irish Cup final	Sat. 13th and	
		Sun. 14th	Anglo-Welsh Cup semi-finals
FEBRUARY 2010		Sun. 14th	FRANCE v ITALY (3.30pm)
Fri. 5th to		Fri. 19th and	
Sun. 7th	English National Championship	Sat. 20th	Welsh Principality Premiership
Sat. 6th	IRELAND v ITALY (2.30pm)	Sat. 20th	WALES v ITALY (2.30pm)
	ENGLAND v WALES (5pm)		IRELAND v SCOTLAND (5pm)
	Anglo-Welsh Cup (4)		FRANCE v ENGLAND (8.45pm)
	Scottish Hydro Premier Cup (1)		English Nat. Lges 1, 2N & S
	Scottish Hydro Nat. Shield (1)	Sat. 20th and	
	Scottish Hydro Regional Bowl (2)	Sun. 21st	Anglo-Welsh Cup final
	Welsh Principality Premiership	Fri. 26th	Magners Celtic League (14)
	Swalec Welsh Nat. Lges E, W	Fri. 26th to	
Sun. 7th	SCOTLAND v FRANCE (3pm)	Sun. 28th	Guinness English Premiership
Fri. 12th to		Sat. 27th	English Nat. Lges 1, 2N & S
Sun. 14th	British & Irish Cup (3)		Scottish Hydro Premier Cup qf
Sat. 13th	WALES v SCOTLAND (2pm)		Scottish Hydro Nat. Shield qf
	FRANCE v IRELAND (5pm)		Scottish Hydro Regional Bowl qf
	English Nat. Lges 1, 2N & S		Swalec Welsh Nat. Lges E, W, N
	Welsh Principality Premiership		Swalec Cup quarter-finals
Sat. 13th and			Swalec Plate quarter-finals
Sun. 14th	Guinness English Premiership		Swalec Bowl quarter-finals
Sun. 14th	ITALY v ENGLAND (3.30pm)		AIB Irish Leagues
Fri. 19th	Magners Celtic League (12)		Under 20 Championship qf
Fri. 19th to		Mon. 29th	Guinness 'A' League
Sun. 21st	Guinness English Premiership	
Sat. 20th	English National Championship	**APRIL 2010**
	English Nat. Lges 1, 2N & S	Fri. 2nd	Magners Celtic League (15)
	Scottish Hydro Prem/ship 1-3	Fri. 2nd to	
	Scottish Hydro Nat. Lges 1-3	Sun. 4th	Guinness English Premiership
	Swalec Welsh Nat. Lge N		

Sat. 3rd	English Nat. Lges 1, 2N & S
	Scottish Hydro Premier Cup sf
	Scottish Hydro Nat. Shield sf
	Scottish Hydro Regional Bowl sf
	Welsh Principality Premiership
	Swalec Welsh Nat. Lges E, W, N
Mon. 5th	Guinness 'A' League
Thu. 8th to	
Sun. 11th	European Challenge Cup qf
Fri. 9th to	
Sun. 11th	Heineken Cup quarter-finals
Sat. 10th	English Nat. Lges 1, 2N & S
	Welsh Principality Premiership
	Swalec Welsh Nat. Lges E, W, N
	AIB Irish Leagues
Mon. 12th	Guinness 'A' League
Fri. 16th	Magners Celtic League (16)
Sat. 17th	English Nat. Lges 2N & S
	Swalec Welsh Nat. Lges E, W, N
	Swalec Cup semi-finals
	Swalec Plate semi-finals
	Swalec Bowl semi-finals
	AIB Irish Leagues semi-finals
	Under 20 Championship sf
Sat. 17th and	
Sun. 18th	Guinness English Premiership
Mon. 19th	Guinness 'A' League
Fri. 23rd	Magners Celtic League (17)
Fri. 23rd to	
Sun. 25th	Guinness English Premiership
	British & Irish Cup semi-finals
Sat. 24th	English Nat. Lges 1, 2N & S
	Scottish Hydro Prem. Cup final
	Scottish Hydro Nat. Shield final
	Scottish Hydro Reg. Bowl final
	Swalec Welsh Nat. Lges E, W, N
Tue. 27th	Welsh Principality Premiership
	Play-off Championship
Fri. 30th to	
Sun. 2nd May	*European Challenge Cup sf

MAY 2010

Sat. 1st	English National Ch/ship final
	County Championship Shield (1)
	Under 20 Championship final

Sat. 1st and	
Sun. 2nd	Heineken Cup semi-finals
Wed. 5th	Welsh Principality Premiership
	Play-off Championship
Fri. 7th	Magners Celtic League (18)
Sat. 8th	Guinness English Premiership
	Bill Beaumont Cup (1)
	County Championship Shield (2)
	County Championship Plate (1)
	Swalec Cup final
	Swalec Plate final
	Swalec Bowl final
	AIB Irish Leagues finals
Wed. 12th	Welsh Principality Premiership
	Play-off Championship
Fri. 14th to	
Sun. 16th	*British & Irish Cup final
Sat. 15th and	Guinness English Premiership sf
Sun. 16th	*Magners Celtic League sf
	Bill Beaumont Cup (2)
	County Championship Shield (3)
	County Championship Plate (2)
Fri. 21st to	
Sun. 23rd	*European Challenge Cup final
Sat. 22nd	Heineken Cup final
	Bill Beaumont Cup (3)
	County Championship Shield sf
	County Championship Plate (3)
Sun. 23rd	Welsh Principality Premiership
	Play-off Ch/ship final
Sat. 29th	Guinness English
	Premiership final
	Bill Beaumont Cup final
	County Ch/ship Shield final
	County Ch/ship Plate final
	*Magners League final

* = Exact dates and times to be confirmed.

Mission Statement

Wooden Spoon aims to enhance the quality and
prospect of life for children and young persons in the
United Kingdom who are presently disadvantaged either
physically, mentally or socially

Charity Registration No: 326691

next

We are proud to support **The Wooden Spoon Rugby Worl**

www.next.co.u